P9-EJT-834

Speed Reading

FOR

DUMMIES®

by Richard Sutz

with Peter Weverka

WILEY

John Wiley & Sons, Inc.

Speed Reading For Dummies®

Published by
John Wiley & Sons, Inc.
111 River St.
Hoboken, NJ 07030-5774
www.wiley.com

Copyright © 2009 by John Wiley & Sons, Inc., Hoboken, New Jersey

Published by John Wiley & Sons, Inc., Hoboken, New Jersey

Published simultaneously in Canada

No part of this publication may be reproduced, stored in a retrieval system or transmitted in any form or by any means, electronic, mechanical, photocopying, recording, scanning or otherwise, except as permitted under Sections 107 or 108 of the 1976 United States Copyright Act, without either the prior written permission of the Publisher, or authorization through payment of the appropriate per-copy fee to the Copyright Clearance Center, 222 Rosewood Drive, Danvers, MA 01923, (978) 750-8400, fax (978) 646-8600. Requests to the Publisher for permission should be addressed to the Permissions Department, John Wiley & Sons, Inc., 111 River Street, Hoboken, NJ 07030, (201) 748-6011, fax (201) 748-6008, or online at http://www.wiley.com/go/permissions.

Trademarks: Wiley, the Wiley logo, For Dummies, the Dummies Man logo, A Reference for the Rest of Us!, The Dummies Way, Dummies Daily, The Fun and Easy Way, Dummies.com, Making Everything Easier, and related trade dress are trademarks or registered trademarks of John Wiley & Sons, Inc. and/or its affiliates in the United States and other countries, and may not be used without written permission. All other trademarks are the property of their respective owners. John Wiley & Sons, Inc., is not associated with any product or vendor mentioned in this book.

LIMIT OF LIABILITY/DISCLAIMER OF WARRANTY: THE PUBLISHER AND THE AUTHOR MAKE NO REPRESENTATIONS OR WARRANTIES WITH RESPECT TO THE ACCURACY OR COMPLETENESS OF THE CONTENTS OF THIS WORK AND SPECIFICALLY DISCLAIM ALL WARRANTIES, INCLUDING WITHOUT LIMITATION WARRANTIES OF FITNESS FOR A PARTICULAR PURPOSE. NO WARRANTY MAY BE CREATED OR EXTENDED BY SALES OR PROMOTIONAL MATERIALS. THE ADVICE AND STRATEGIES CONTAINED HEREIN MAY NOT BE SUITABLE FOR EVERY SITUATION. THIS WORK IS SOLD WITH THE UNDERSTANDING THAT THE PUBLISHER IS NOT ENGAGED IN RENDERING LEGAL, ACCOUNTING, OR OTHER PROFESSIONAL SERVICES. IF PROFESSIONAL ASSISTANCE IS REQUIRED, THE SERVICES OF A COMPETENT PROFESSIONAL PERSON SHOULD BE SOUGHT. NEITHER THE PUBLISHER NOR THE AUTHOR SHALL BE LIABLE FOR DAMAGES ARISING HEREFROM. THE FACT THAT AN ORGANIZATION OR WEBSITE IS REFERRED TO IN THIS WORK AS A CITATION AND/OR A POTENTIAL SOURCE OF FURTHER INFORMATION DOES NOT MEAN THAT THE AUTHOR OR THE PUBLISHER ENDORSES THE INFORMATION THE ORGANIZATION OR WEBSITE MAY PROVIDE OR RECOMMENDATIONS IT MAY MAKE. FURTHER, READERS SHOULD BE AWARE THAT INTERNET WEBSITES LISTED IN THIS WORK MAY HAVE CHANGED OR DISAPPEARED BETWEEN WHEN THIS WORK WAS WRITTEN AND WHEN IT IS READ.

For general information on our other products and services, please contact our Customer Care Department within the U.S. at 877-762-2974, outside the U.S. at 317-572-3993, or fax 317-572-4002.

For technical support, please visit www.wiley.com/techsupport.

Wiley publishes in a variety of print and electronic formats and by print-on-demand. Some material included with standard print versions of this book may not be included in e-books or in print-on-demand. If this book refers to media such as a CD or DVD that is not included in the version you purchased, you may download this material at http://booksupport.wiley.com. For more information about Wiley products, visit www.wiley.com.

Library of Congress Control Number: 2009928739

ISBN 978-0-470-45744-3 (pbk); ISBN 978-0-470-55051-9 (ebk); ISBN 978-0-470-55052-6 (ebk); ISBN 978-0-470-55053-3 (ebk)

Manufactured in the United States of America

10 9 8 7 6 5

WILEY

About the Authors

Richard Sutz is founder of The Literacy Company. The company's software, The Reader's Edge, is the result of more than $3 million of research and development. Richard began his involvement in speed reading more than 30 years ago as a consultant to and a personal friend of Evelyn Wood, the speed-reading pioneer. His background and experience span executive roles in both the private and public sector. Richard was Grumman Aircraft's Assistant Director for Europe and the Middle East. In the late 1970s, he was appointed Deputy Director of the Arizona Energy Office and later joined the U.S. Department of Energy as director of the Energy Related Inventions Program.

Peter Weverka is the author of many *For Dummies* books, including *Office 2007 All-in-One Desk Reference For Dummies.* His articles and stories have appeared in *Harper's, SPY,* and other magazines.

Dedication

This book is dedicated to the pioneers, researchers, teachers, and entrepreneurs who from 1880 to the present have provided a solid base upon which to build my company's innovative, award-winning program that teaches silent reading fluency. I'm proud to bring their teachings into the 21st century.

Author's Acknowledgements

Where to begin? First with my wife, Wink Blair, who has been a solid rock of support during the years that I've spent on my entrepreneurial ventures. I thank her from the bottom of my heart.

I thank my second family too. My partners in The Literacy Company (TLC): Rich Coppola, the co-developer of TLC's technology, and Lance Leishman, TLC's Operations Manager, ran the company while I was engaged in researching and writing this book.

A special thanks goes to Wiley Publishing for giving me the opportunity to present what I believe will be a road map to change the nation's reading curriculum. I want to thank Michael Lewis for his support and for understanding that there is a world of difference between subject matter knowledge, which I do have, and the ability to write a *For Dummies* book, which I do not have. Michael arranged for me to have the very best professional writer, Peter Weverka, work with me. Without Peter's partnership, this book could not have been written. Also at Wiley, I want to thank Alissa Schwipps and Megan Knoll. It's incredibly eye-opening to observe the enormous improvements made by professional editing. I take my hat off to them.

I also want to thank Bill Cowles of SkillPath Seminars and Tom Hopkins International for being early adopters of silent reading instruction as taught by The Reader's Edge. I thank the thousands of individuals, schools, colleges, universities, and corporations in 99 countries who now use The Reader's Edge to learn efficient and effective speed-reading skills.

Finally, I want to thank Harvey Mackay, Tom Hopkins, Rogers Historical Museum, and StrugglingReaders.com for permitting me to use their columns and essays in this book as reading selections. I thank Evan Islam for his list of Fortune Cookies Sayings and Idiomsite.com and UsingEnglish.com for their list of idioms. I also thank Howard Bailey for permitting me to use the Recognition and Motility Eye exercises in this book.

Publisher's Acknowledgments

We're proud of this book; please send us your comments through our Dummies online registration form located at http://dummies.custhelp.com. For other comments, please contact our Customer Care Department within the U.S. at 877-762-2974, outside the U.S. at 317-572-3993, or fax 317-572-4002.

Some of the people who helped bring this book to market include the following:

Acquisitions, Editorial, and Media Development

Senior Project Editor: Alissa Schwipps

Acquisitions Editor: Michael Lewis

Copy Editor: Megan Knoll

Assistant Editor: Erin Calligan Mooney

Editorial Program Coordinator: Joe Niesen

Technical Editor: Ed Caldwell

Senior Editorial Manager: Jennifer Ehrlich

Editorial Assistants: Jennette ElNaggar, David Lutton

Cover Photo: Walter B. McKenzie

Cartoons: Rich Tennant (www.the5thwave.com)

Composition Services

Project Coordinator: Lynsey Stanford

Layout and Graphics: Reuben W. Davis, Christine Williams, Erin Zeltner

Proofreader: Jennifer Theriot

Indexer: Potomac Indexing, LLC

Publishing and Editorial for Consumer Dummies

   Kathleen Nebenhaus, Vice President and Executive Publisher

   David Palmer, Associate Publisher

   Kristin Ferguson-Wagstaffe, Product Development Director

Publishing for Technology Dummies

   Andy Cummings, Vice President and Publisher

Composition Services

   Debbie Stailey, Director of Composition Services

Contents at a Glance

Table of Contents

Part III: Advancing Your Speed-Reading Skills 125

Chapter 8: Building Your Speed-Reading Momentum 127

Chapter 9: Exercising Your Ability to Read More in Even Less Time 147

Chapter 10: Other Reading Strategies to Supplement Your Speed Reading 165

Introduction

No matter how quickly or slowly you read now, you can read much more rapidly by adopting the speed-reading techniques described in this book. You can also comprehend, retain, and recall what you read much more successfully. You can become an efficient and effective reader, one who reads with confidence and greater understanding. You can read more in the time you devote to reading and get more from the articles and books you read.

This book represents all that I know and have discovered about speed reading during my 40 years as a speed-reading instructor and developer of speed-reading software. I have had the great pleasure of seeing my students' reading speeds and comprehension improve dramatically, and I have also seen them derive greater pleasure from reading. These goals — increasing your reading speed and your pleasure from reading — are what this book is all about.

About This Book

The science (some would say art) of speed reading is about 100 years old. Consequently, theories abound as to what makes a good speed reader and how to become a speed reader. This book takes a very basic approach to the subject — I believe speed reading is efficient reading. You don't have to be a wizard or master arcane techniques to be a speed reader. All you have to do is understand the mechanics of reading and then apply yourself more efficiently to exercising those mechanics when you read. This book shows you how to do that.

Speed Reading For Dummies is for people who have little or no background in speed reading, as well as for experienced speed readers who want to hone their speed-reading skills. It offers many strategies, tips, and tricks to improve your reading speed and includes numerous exercises to give you hands-on practice in speed-reading techniques. It also explains the how and why of speed-reading mechanics so that you understand not just what to do when you speed read but also why you do it.

A note about the exercises: If at first you don't succeed, try again. Everyone grasps new material at a different rate — don't get discouraged if you don't do as well as you expect the first time out of the gate. You can apply these exercises to just about any reading material to get additional practice; as I mention elsewhere in this book, newspapers are perfect for speed-reading practice, so consider starting there.

You don't have to read this book from start to finish — unless you want to, of course. I wrote and organized *Speed Reading For Dummies* so that you can start reading it anywhere you want. Consult the table of contents or "How This Book Is Organized" later in this introduction to find the speed-reading topic that interests you.

Conventions Used in This Book

To make this book easier to read, I've adopted these conventions:

- ✔ I *italicize* new terms in the text the first time I introduce them and then follow them closely with an easy-to-understand definition.

- ✔ Steps in the exercises are numbered and appear in **boldface** text. Follow the boldface instructions to complete the exercises.

- ✔ Web addresses appear in `monofont`.

- ✔ Though many use the term *vocalization* to mean "reading aloud," for the purposes of this book I define vocalization as "speaking or hearing words as you read them."

- ✔ Some exercises include long text pieces for you to practice on. I label these pieces to correspond with the exercise number (so Practice Text 7-1 goes with Exercise 7-1). For exercises that have multiple text pieces (such as those that ask you to read the same essay in different formats), I add a letter to each Practice Text heading (for example, Practice Text 2-1a and Practice Text 2-1b).

What You're Not to Read

I've written this book so you can find the information you need easily and quickly. All the chapters provide you with important information, but the sidebars offer greater detail or tidbits of information that you can skip if you like. I encourage you to read this information along with the regular text, but if you want to focus on the main points of the chapters, you can always come back to these shaded sections another time.

Foolish Assumptions

Forgive me, but I've made a few foolish assumptions about you, the reader of this book. I assume the following:

✔ You want to read anything and everything more quickly.

✔ You want to better comprehend and retain the books, articles, and Web pages you read every day.

✔ You feel overwhelmed by the amount of info you have to read for work or school and want a way to quickly and effectively get through all of it.

✔ You've heard a few tidbits about speed reading and are intrigued by the topic or wonder whether what you've heard is true.

✔ You want a plainspoken guide that trains you to speed read without a lot of fuss so you can quickly master speed-reading techniques.

How This Book Is Organized

Following is a short summary of each part of *Speed Reading For Dummies*. I invite you to use this summary as a quick guide to speed reading topics that interest you. Choose the speed-reading topic that interests you and have at it.

Part 1: Introducing Speed Reading

Part I lays the groundwork for understanding what speed reading is and how you can read more efficiently. Chapter 1 explains what happens in your brain and other parts of your anatomy when you speed read and the skills you need to be a speed reader. Chapter 2 delves into two bad habits — vocalizing and regressing — that keep you from reading quickly and then shows you how to break these habits. In Chapter 3, I look into eye fixations, vision span, and other reading mechanics to help you understand how to be a speed reader. Chapter 4 offers a number of speed reading exercises to give you a sense of the different skills you need to develop (and can develop with the exercises in Part II).

Part II: Focusing on the Fundamentals

Part II explores the core fundamentals of speed reading. First, Chapter 5 gives you an opportunity to take your first speed-reading tests so that you know where you stand. Then in Chapter 6 you take your first steps down the road to reading more than one word at a time as you discover how to widen your vision span vertically and horizontally when you read. Chapter 7 gives you practice in reading for units of meaning so that you read not only more than one word at a time but also one entire thought at a time and increase your comprehension, retention, and recall.

Part III: Advancing Your Speed-Reading Skills

Part III takes you to a higher speed-reading realm. To reinforce your speed-reading skills, Chapter 8 offers exercises that have you read text in ever wider columns so you can challenge your ability to read more words per eye fixation. Chapter 9 presents techniques to help you read aggressively with heightened concentration. In Chapter 10, you go above and beyond the normal speed-reading skills — this chapter explains how to skim, scan, and preread. Chapter 11 explains some refined speed-reading skills, including how to recognize the essence of a paragraph, follow the author's thought patterns, and skip subordinate clauses in your reading.

Part IV: Improving Your Comprehension

Part IV looks at how to improve your comprehension, retention, and recall. Because having a large vocabulary is essential to being a speed reader, Chapter 12 shows how to expand your vocabulary. Chapter 13 explores a potpourri of speed-reading tasks, including encouraging children to speed read; speed reading standardized tests, textbooks, and newspapers; and increasing your reading pleasure.

Part V: The Part of Tens

Each of the chapters in Part V offers advice for being a better speed reader. Chapter 14 offers quick tips for improving your speed reading. Chapter 15 presents eye exercises for expanding your reading vision and seeing after your eye health, and Chapter 16 shows you how to make your speed reading skills permanent.

Part VI: Appendixes

You thought you were done, right? Not so fast — Part VI offers two appendixes. Appendix A lists the 2,000 most common words in the English language so you can be sure you know these all-important words. Appendix B provides a worksheet to help you track your progress on various exercises in this book.

Icons Used in This Book

To help you get the most out of this book, I've placed icons here and there. Here's what the icons mean:

Next to the Tip icon, you find tricks of the trade designed to make you a better speed reader.

Where you see the Warning icon, tread carefully: These icons alert you to common speed-reading mistakes and errors.

Remember icons mark juicy facts that bear remembering. When you see this icon, prick up your ears.

Where to Go from Here

Where should you start reading? Anywhere your curiosity takes you. However, a couple of good starting points are Chapter 2, which describes bad reading habits you must overcome to be a speed reader, and Chapter 3, which looks at the mechanics of speed reading. Wherever you start, good luck in your speed-reading adventures!

Part I
Introducing Speed Reading

The 5th Wave   By Rich Tennant

"In order to work on your eye fixations I'm pretty sure they have to be in the 'open' position."

In this part...

With the idea that you should look before you leap, Part I provides a general introduction to speed reading. These chapters explain what goes on in your mind and body during the act of speed reading, what skills every speed reader needs, and which bad reading habits you need to break if you want to be a speed reader.

If you're new to speed reading, I suggest reading all of Part I, especially Chapter 1, which describes the anatomy of reading, and Chapter 2, which explains why vocalization is a hindrance to fast reading and how to break the vocalization habit. Chapter 3 shows how to expand your vision and take in several words at once in the act of reading. Visit Chapter 4 to get a taste of the different skills you need to acquire to become a speed reader.

Chapter 1

Of Course You Can Speed Read!

*I*f you're a typical reader, your reading education ended in the third grade, and you currently read using the same techniques you used as a third grader. You're not reading as fast as you want because no one taught you the skills to read faster.

That's the bad news.

The good news is that everybody can increase their reading speed by adopting a few simple techniques. Beyond those techniques, by being a committed reader, applying speed-reading principles, and reading with more concentration, you can read very quickly — perhaps doubling or even tripling your current reading speed. You can also read with better comprehension and retain and recall what you read. What's more, you can get more pleasure and meaning from the books, articles, and Web pages you read.

This chapter introduces basic speed-reading concepts and demonstrates why anyone can become a speed reader. At the end of the chapter, you can find an exercise that lets you put speed-reading skills to the test and see for yourself just how helpful a few techniques can be.

What Is Speed Reading, Anyway?

When you read the words on the page of a book or newspaper article, what goes on in your head? Do you also hear the words as you read them? If you do, someone is speaking them, and unless a leprechaun is sitting on your shoulder, that someone is you.

Reading engages the eyes, ears, mouth, and, of course, the brain. Speed reading engages these senses even more than normal reading because you use your senses and brain power even more efficiently. The following sections explain in detail what goes on in your eyes, ears, mouth, and brain when you speed read.

Speed reading is seeing

First and foremost, speed reading is seeing; the first step in reading anything is seeing the words. But how do you see words on the page when you read?

Prior to 1920 or so, researchers and educators believed that people read one word at a time. To read, they thought, you moved your eyes left to right across the page, taking in one word after the other. Under this theory, fast readers were people who could identify and recognize the words faster.

However, all but beginning readers have the ability to see and read more than one word at a time. As you move your eyes left to right across the page, you jump ahead in fits and starts, taking in anywhere between one and five words at a time in quick glances.

These quick glances, when your eyes stop moving at different points in a sentence as you read it, are called *eye fixations*. I get into more detail on how eye fixations work in Chapter 3, but for now, the important points to know about speed reading are

- ✔ **You read several words in a single glance.** Unless you're encountering words you don't know or haven't read before, you don't read words one at a time.

- ✔ **You expand your vision so that you can read and understand many words in a single glance.** A very good speed reader can read, see, and process 10 to 14 words in a single eye fixation.

- ✔ **You expand your vision to read vertically as well as horizontally on the page.** As well as taking in more than one word on a line of text, speed readers can also, in a single glance, read and understand words on two or three different lines. Check out Chapter 6 for more on expanding your reading vision, and head to Chapter 15 for some exercises that help you do just that.

Speed reading is silent reading

When you read, do you sometimes hear a faint whispering in your ear that belongs not to you, but to another person? Don't fret, because you aren't alone. Most people hear words when they read. The words speak to them from the page.

When you read, you speak words to yourself because you learned to read with the sound-it-out method. In school, your teacher told you that each letter makes a sound (sometimes more than one sound), that certain letter combinations also make sounds, and that you can always read a word by sounding out the letters and letter combinations:

> su-per-cal-i-frag-il-ist-ic-ex-pi-al-i-do-cious

Your teacher was absolutely right. Being able to sound out words is an essential skill for beginning readers. Knowing the sounds each letter makes and knowing what sounds letter combinations make enables you to pronounce and read any word you encounter in your reading.

The problem with the sound-it-out approach to reading is that it slows you down. You read not at the speed you think but rather at the speed you talk. Sounding it out is fine for beginning readers, but at some point you have to dispense with sound if you want to be a speed reader. Saying the words, even if you only whisper them inside the confines of your skull, takes time.

In speed-reading terminology, saying and hearing words as you read them is called *vocalizing* (Chapter 2 gives you the lowdown on vocalizing and how to stop it). For now you need to remember that

✔ Vocalizing is a throwback to your early reading education; you must abandon it to be a speed reader.

✔ Training yourself not to vocalize when you read is one of the most important speed-reading skills you can acquire.

Speed reading is decoding the words

When you come across a word in your reading that you don't know or recognize, you have to decode it. You break it into syllables, try to pronounce it, and see whether it's related to words you know. You try to get its meaning, and if you can't do that on your own, you consult a dictionary or other reference source.

Beginning readers have to decode most of the words they encounter. But the more you read, the fewer words you have to decode because reading enlarges your vocabulary. It introduces you to more words.

Chapter 12 explains how to enlarge your vocabulary. For now, all you need to know about speed reading is

- ✔ The larger your vocabulary is, the faster you can read, because you don't have to slow down or halt your reading as often to decode words you don't know.

- ✔ If you want to be a speed reader, you have to develop your vocabulary.

Speed reading is comprehending

The purpose of reading is to comprehend — to learn something new, see the world from a different perspective, or maybe just get information to pass an exam or prepare for a business meeting.

How well you comprehend what you read is determined by these factors:

- ✔ **Reading speed:** When you don't read at the right speed, your comprehension is diminished. One of the skills you acquire as a speed reader is knowing when to slow down and when to speed up. The fastest speed readers adjust the speed at which they read, just as the fastest stock car racers slow down when they're in a crowded field or on a slick patch of roadway. They adjust their speed according to the type of reading they're doing.

- ✔ **Breadth of vocabulary:** Having a large vocabulary is a must for speed readers. You can't get away from it.

- ✔ **Degree of familiarity with the subject matter:** How strong a background you have in the topic you're reading about determines how well you comprehend what you read. Obviously, you have a head start if you're traveling in territory you're familiar with and you know the jargon already.

Though many chapters in this book deal with comprehension in some aspect, Part IV (Chapters 12 and 13) deals specifically with improving your comprehension as you speed read. At this point, what you need to know about speed reading is that

- ✔ **Speed reading actually increases reading comprehension.** Because you read several words at a time when you speed read, you can pick up the meaning of words in context. This ability to read in context improves comprehension because each word in the sentence gives meaning to the other words instead of standing alone.

✔ **Speed reading has a snowball effect on the size of your vocabulary and general knowledge, which increases your reading speed.** The more you read, the larger your vocabulary and breadth of knowledge become; the larger they become, the more easily you read, which encourages you to read more and broaden your vocabulary and knowledge.

✔ **You can adopt many strategies for improving your comprehension when you read.** For example, you can train yourself to pinpoint the most important parts of an essay and read them more carefully. You can even focus on the most important parts of a sentence as you read them. In Chapter 13, I describe strategies for reading efficiently to complete various kinds of tasks.

Speed reading is concentrating

All reading requires concentration; even reading a third-rate thriller on the beach on a beautiful sunny day requires a certain amount of concentration. If only for a moment, you have to ignore the refreshing breeze, as enticing as it feels, to find out whether the hero will escape from the villain's secret mountaintop retreat.

Speed reading, however, requires sustained, forceful concentration because when you speed read, you do many things at once. As you see and read the words on the page, you also remain alert to the main ideas that the author wants to present. You have to think along with the author and detect how she presents the material so you can pin down the main ideas. As you read, you have to read with more perspective and separate the details from weightier stuff. You have to know when to skim, when to read fast, and when to slow down to get the gist of it. (Chapter 10 helps you choose your reading speed.)

Speed reading also requires you to read aggressively. You read hungrily, absorbing the information as you come to it.

One way to improve your concentration when you speed read is to imagine that nothing exists outside the boundaries of the page you're reading (or the boundaries of the monitor, if you're reading at your computer). Pretend that the entire universe has been condensed to the square space in front of your nose. Nothing can distract you because nothing exists to distract you.

Debunking Speed-Reading Myths

The previous section explains what reading, and speed reading in particular, is. This section explains what speed reading isn't. These myths about speed reading are false:

- ✔ **You don't enjoy reading as much when you speed read.** On the contrary! Speed reading is efficient reading, as I explain in "What Is Speed Reading, Anyway?" earlier in this chapter. When you speed read, you're a better reader — you get more pleasure and meaning out of the books, articles, and Web pages that you read. In my years as a speed-reading teacher, I have seen countless individuals grow to love reading after they learned how to speed read.

- ✔ **You don't comprehend as well when you speed read.** Speed reading is the act of reading with higher levels of concentration. What's more, by reading several words at a time rather than one word after the other, your comprehension increases. You can read words in context and derive more meaning from the words you read. Check out "Speed reading is comprehending" earlier in this chapter for more on why this myth is a sham.

- ✔ **You skip words when you speed read.** Wrong again. Speed readers don't fixate their eyes on all the words as they read, but that doesn't mean they skip the words. Speed reading entails reading words in clumps, or groups. You read more than one word at a time, but no word gets skipped. (Head to Chapter 6 for more on reading word clumps.)

- ✔ **You have to run your finger down the page or use a pacer when you speed read.** A *pacer* is a visual guide, such as your finger or a pen, that marks where you read on the page. Most people have a stereotypical image of a speed reader as a crazed-looking individual dragging her finger or a pacer quickly down the page in the act of reading. However, you don't *need* a pacer to speed read. As I explain in Chapter 3, a pacer can be helpful in the early stages of speed reading, but you're wise to abandon it after you get the hang of speed reading.

What You Need to Get Started

Besides the ability to concentrate, you don't need very much to speed read.

If you're reading a book, magazine, newspaper, or the like, you need a quiet, well-lit place free from noise and other distractions. Make wherever you can concentrate best the place you go when you want to speed read.

You may also use a pacer when you read. (Chapter 3 discusses pacers in detail.) A *pacer* is a reading aid such as a card or your hand that directs you where to look on the page when you read. In the exercises, I sometimes call on you to use a pacer; choose a pacer that's most comfortable for you.

Some of the exercises in this book call for you to time your reading speed. If you have a stopwatch you can use to time yourself, great. If not, you need a clock or watch with a second hand so you can time yourself down to the second.

Don't look at your clock or watch while you do the exercises! You may distract yourself from getting the highest possible score.

You also need a good pair of eyes, and barring that, a good pair of glasses. How's your eyesight? No matter how good or poor it is, flip to Chapter 15 for some eye exercises that improve the health of your eyes and Chapter 16 for more info on the importance of good eye health.

When you speed read, you should be comfortable, but not too comfortable. For example, a hammock isn't a good location for speed reading. Hammocks induce sleep, not higher levels of concentration.

More than ever, people do their reading on computer monitors, not the pages of books, newspapers, or magazines. You can do a handful of things to make computer reading more comfortable and less of a strain on your eyes. Check out Chapter 13 for advice.

Proving You Can Read Faster

In "What Is Speed Reading, Anyway?" earlier in this chapter, I explain both the disadvantages of vocalizing and the benefits of using eye fixations as you read. Exercise 1-1 demonstrates these points. In this exercise, you read a short essay called "The Need to Revise the Nation's Reading Curriculum" twice. You read it first without the benefits of the speed-reading principles I cover in this chapter, and then you put on your speed-reading cap and read the essay again, using basic speed-reading techniques. At the end of the exercise, you compare reading times.

Follow these steps to complete the first half of the exercise:

1. **Take note of the time you start reading.**

2. **Read the following presentation of "The Need to Revise the Nation's Reading Curriculum" (Practice Text 1-1a) out loud.**

   That's right — say every single word, pronouncing each word carefully and correctly. Speak loud enough to make the dog or cat (if one is in the room) prick up his ears. Reading aloud like this requires you to read one word at a time, which is what happens when you vocalize.

3. **When you finish reading, write down how long it took to read the essay on the worksheet in Appendix B.**

Practice Text 1-1a

The Need to Revise the Nation's Reading Curriculum
by Richard Sutz

Call to action: To revise the nation's reading curriculum in order to create a more literate society where the potential and productivity of the citizenry is not limited or constrained by ineffective, slow reading. This revision is needed because formal reading education, the learn-to-read stage, officially *stops* after third grade, at which time children have learned:

- *Only* to read one word at a time, out loud — what we call "oral reading fluency."

- *None* of the necessary read-to-learn skills — what we call "silent reading fluency."

We propose four revisions to the nation's reading curriculum that incorporate teaching children the silent reading skills necessary to become effective and efficient readers. To achieve silent reading fluency, children must be taught to see, read, and process groups of words or units of meaning with each eye fixation, without vocalizing (lip or subliminally).

1. REVISE the No Child Left Behind Act goals to redefine oral reading fluency as the *interim goal,* and incorporate silent reading fluency as the *new end-goal.*

2. TRAIN educators to teach silent reading skills to children before, during, and after third grade.

Practice Text 1-1a *(continued)*

---

3. REQUIRE mastery of prime words (approximately 75 percent of all words found in print). This will dramatically facilitate reading groups of words automatically, with improved comprehension, while reading silently.

4. ASSESS reading improvement in standardized testing related to the teaching of silent reading skills.

These revisions will *guarantee* successful teaching, learning, and mastery of silent reading skills — skills that are required in today's information-based society where all reading is silent and individuals are judged on their ability to read to learn.

About USA's Current Reading Curriculum — The Good Side: No Child Left Behind set a standard and timeline by which all of the nation's children will demonstrate that they have learned to read by the end of third grade. The benefits of early reading education are indisputable. Children who are literate (who can read and enjoy reading) are better equipped to avoid drugs, teen suicide, and dropping out of high school, and 90 percent of learning is based on reading. Children who cannot read by the end of third grade are far more likely to be school dropouts, experience teen-age pregnancy, rely on state social services as adults, and be forced into low-skill, low-wage jobs throughout their lives.

About USA's Current Reading Curriculum — The Bad Side: Children are not explicitly taught effective and efficient fluent silent reading skills. Why? Because formal reading education stops *immediately* after oral reading skills are mastered. Hence, fourth graders, armed only with oral reading skills (the exact opposite of silent reading skills) enter the silent reading world unprepared to read to learn. They are condemned to become slow readers. As a result:

- Students in the fourth grade will continue to experience the well-known "fourth grade slump" — universally understood to be caused by poor reading skills.

- Poor readers in elementary school will continue to become poorer readers in high school and enter adulthood lacking minimal levels of reading skills necessary to achieve successful lives and careers.

- Our nation will continue to create poor readers with all the negative issues associated with a citizenry unable to read efficiently. (Arizona and other states utilize fourth grade reading assessment results as one basis for long-term projections of how many prison beds will be required.)

(continued)

Practice Text 1-1a *(continued)*

Why Does Formal Reading Education Stop after Third Grade?
Because the "end goal" of the current reading curriculum,
per No Child Left Behind, is to have children read at the third
grade level by the end of third grade, producing children who
are only skilled as fluent oral readers. Federal funding supporting reading-to-learn education is *drastically* reduced after third
grade; hence, silent reading skills are not taught.

The Solution: Oral reading fluency should be redefined as the
No Child Left Behind Act's interim-goal of reading education.
The Act's end-goal should now be defined as requiring students to demonstrate mastery of silent reading skills — seeing,
reading, and processing more than one word at a time without
vocalizing (lip or subliminally).

Technology to Accomplish the Solution: Our company utilizes
scientifically sound principles to dramatically teach how to
unlearn the habits of slow readers (oral readers) and learn
the habits and skills used by fluent readers (silent readers).
Mastering silent reading skills arms children, as well as adults,
with skills needed in the real world, where all reading is done
silently.

How Long Does It Take to Learn Silent Reading Skills? Our company guarantees that individuals of any age can double their
reading speed with increased comprehension and recall by
spending a minimum of 15 minutes every other day for three
weeks with our software. Greater improvement will come with
additional practice.

When you read the selection a second time, take to heart these
speed-reading basics:

- **Read aggressively.** Part of being a speed reader is reading with
  more intensity, focus, and concentration. This time, devour the
  words as you read them. Be an active, not a passive, reader.

- **Don't vocalize.** As best you can, glance at the words and take
  in their meaning without hearing them. (Chapter 2 offers techniques to keep from vocalizing.)

- **Widen your vision.** Instead of focusing on a word at a time,
  focus on four, seven, or ten words. Trust yourself to be able
  to see the most relevant words at a glance and fill in the rest.

Follow these steps to complete the second half of Exercise 1-1:

1. **Take note of the time you start reading the second presentation of "The Need to Revise the Nation's Reading
   Curriculum" (Practice Text 1-1b).**

2. **Read the following presentation of the essay silently; try to resist the urge to vocalize.**

   Notice how this second presentation is divided into one- to five-word clumps. You're now reading the essay as a speed reader would read it. You aren't vocalizing, and you're reading several words at a time. Notice how much faster you read.

3. **When you finish reading the second presentation of the essay, write down how long you took to read it in Appendix B and compare your first reading time to your second reading time.**

Practice Text 1-1b

The Need to Revise the Nation's Reading Curriculum

Call to action:

To revise

the nation's reading curriculum

in order to create

a more literate society

where the potential

and productivity

of the citizenry

is not limited

or constrained

by ineffective, slow reading.

This revision is needed

because formal reading education,

the learn-to-read stage,

officially *stops*

after third grade,

at which time

children have learned:

 • *Only* to read

    one word at a time,

out loud —

what we call

"oral reading fluency."

 • *None* of the necessary

    read-to-learn skills —

    what we call

    "silent reading fluency."

We propose four revisions

to the nation's

reading curriculum

that incorporate

teaching children

the silent reading skills

necessary to become

effective and efficient readers.

To achieve

silent reading fluency,

children must be taught

to see, read, and process

groups of words or

(continued)

Practice Text 1-1b *(continued)*

---

units of meaning
with each eye fixation,
without vocalizing
(lip or subliminally).
1. REVISE the
   No Child Left Behind Act goals
   to redefine oral reading fluency
   as the *interim goal,*
   and incorporate
   silent reading fluency
   as the *new end-goal.*
2. TRAIN educators
   to teach silent reading skills
   to children
   before, during, and after
   third grade.
3. REQUIRE mastery
   of prime words
   (approximately 75 percent
   of all words found in print).
   This will dramatically
   facilitate reading
   groups of words automatically,
   with improved comprehension,
   while reading silently.
4. ASSESS reading improvement
   in standardized testing
   related to the teaching
   of silent reading skills.
These revisions
will *guarantee* successful
teaching, learning, and mastery

of silent reading skills —
skills that are required
in today's
information-based society
where all reading
is silent and
individuals are judged
on their ability to read to learn.
About USA's
Current Reading Curriculum —
The Good Side:
No Child Left Behind set
a standard and timeline
by which all of
the nation's children
will demonstrate that
they have learned to read
by the end of third grade.
The benefits of
early reading education
are indisputable.
Children who are literate
(who can read and enjoy reading)
are better equipped to
avoid drugs, teen suicide, and
dropping out of high school,
and 90 percent of learning
is based on reading.
Children who cannot read
by the end of third grade
are far more likely
to be school dropouts,

Practice Text 1-1b *(continued)*

experience teenage pregnancy,
rely on state social services
as adults,
and be forced into
low-skill, low-wage jobs
throughout their lives.

About USA's
Current Reading Curriculum —
The Bad Side:

Children are not explicitly
taught effective and efficient
fluent silent reading skills.
Why? Because
formal reading education stops
immediately after oral reading skills
are mastered.
Hence, fourth graders,
armed only with oral reading skills
(the exact opposite of silent reading skills)
enter the silent reading world
unprepared to read to learn.
They are condemned
to become slow readers.
As a result:

• Students in the fourth grade
   will continue to experience
   the well-known "fourth grade slump" —
   universally understood
   to be caused by
   poor reading skills.

• Poor readers
   in elementary school
   will continue to become
   poorer readers in high school
   and enter adulthood
   lacking minimal levels of
   reading skills necessary
   to achieve successful lives
   and careers.

• Our nation will
   continue to create
   poor readers with
   all the negative issues
   associated with a citizenry
   unable to read efficiently.
   (Arizona and other states
   utilize fourth grade
   reading assessment results
   as one basis for
   long-term projections
   of how many prison beds
   will be required.)

Why Does
Formal Reading Education
stop after third grade?
Because the "end goal"
of the current reading curriculum,
per No Child Left Behind,
is to have children
read at the third grade level
by the end of third grade,

(continued)

Practice Text 1-1b *(continued)*

---

producing children
who are only skilled
as fluent oral readers.
Federal funding supporting
reading-to-learn education
is *drastically* reduced
after third grade; hence,
silent reading skills
are not taught.
The Solution:
Oral reading fluency
should be redefined
as the No Child Left Behind Act's
interim-goal of reading education.
The Act's end-goal
should now be defined
as requiring students t
o demonstrate mastery
of silent reading skills —
seeing, reading, and processing
more than one word at a time
without vocalizing
(lip or subliminally).
Technology to
Accomplish the Solution:
Our company utilizes

scientifically sound principles to
dramatically teach
how to unlearn the habits
of slow readers (oral readers)
and learn the habits and skills
used by fluent readers
(silent readers).
Mastering silent reading skills
arms children,
as well as adults,
with skills needed
in the real world,
where all reading is done silently.
How Long Does It Take
to Learn Silent Reading Skills?
Our company guarantees
that individuals of any age
can double their reading speed
with increased comprehension
and recall
by spending a minimum of 15 minutes
every other day
for three weeks
with our software.
Greater improvement will
come with additional practice.

If I was a betting man, I'd bet the farm that you read the second presentation faster than the first. Just by reading more aggressively, being careful not to vocalize, and seeing more than one word at a time, you can be a much better reader. The rest of this book gives you many strategies for reading faster, but it all boils down to aggressiveness, silent reading, and better vision.

Chapter 2

It's All about Breaking Bad Reading Habits

....

....

*H*alf of becoming a speed reader is developing new skills; the other half is breaking the bad habits that keep you from reading faster.

This chapter looks at the bad habits side of speed reading. It examines vocalization and explains how you can drop the habit of saying and hearing words as you read. It also explains why some people regress — why they're in the habit of rereading — and how you can dump this habit if you have it.

Understanding Vocalization and Its Effects

Reading educators use the term *vocalization* to describe readers who hear words when they read. Vocalizers are readers who read with their mouths — they say and hear the words as they read. Vocalizing slows your reading down considerably and is a habit you should break if you intend to become a speed reader.

In the following sections, you find out what causes vocalization and how to determine whether you vocalize when you read.

Finding out why vocalizing slows you down

Silently read the following nursery rhyme. As you read, note whether you hear the words in spite of your reading them silently:

Hickory dickory dock

The mouse ran up the clock

The clock struck one

The mouse ran down

Hickory dickory dock

I chose this nursery rhyme because it includes several loud, hard consonants (*k*s and *d*s) that test your ability to read without hearing the words. Did you hear the *k*s, *d*s, and other sounds? If your answer is *no,* you're probably not being entirely truthful. Even fast readers vocalize a little bit.

Vocalizing as little as possible is an essential goal of speed reading. Vocalizing hinders your reading for these reasons:

- ✔ **It slows down your reading.** The average person speaks at 150 to 200 words per minute. If you vocalize all words as you read, you can't read faster than this rate because you have to read the words at the rate you speak them. By contrast, advanced readers read at 200 to 400 words per minute, and speed readers read above 400 words or more per minute.

- ✔ **It affects comprehension.** If you move your lips or mimic speech when you read, you engage a part of your mind in speech activities when you really ought to devote it to grasping the author's ideas.

- ✔ **It hinders your ability to comprehend through context clues.** For example, the first two words of this sentence make no sense until you read the complete sentence: "Sénéchal, bailli — the knight aspired to one of these positions in the royal administration." Readers who vocalize are baffled by the first two words of this sentence and are slow to comprehend them, but fast readers who don't vocalize can read the entire sentence in one or two glances, and they know immediately that the words *sénéchal* and *bailli* refer to administrative positions appointed by the king.

✔ **It causes regression.** As I explain later in this chapter, regression occurs when you're unsure of what you read and you move your eyes backward over words and sentences you have read already to confirm their meaning. Vocalizing causes regression because your eyes race ahead of your mouth in the act of reading, and your mouth reads one place while your eyes read another. This gap between what the mouth says and what the eyes see creates confusion and causes you to regress.

Finding out how (and how much) you vocalize

How you break the vocalization habit depends on how much you vocalize when you read. Try the following test to determine how much you vocalize.

Taking the vocalization test

Read this paragraph to yourself, not aloud. As you read, listen with your ears and also be aware of any movement or feeling in your lips, tongue, vocal cords, larynx (voice box), and throat.

Did you hear the lark singing in the square? I heard it. In fact, it woke me up. Why that little bird chooses to sing at night is a mystery. The lark sings in my dreams and sings when I'm awake. You can't stop that bird from singing!

Tracing the causes of vocalization

It's hard not to vocalize when you read because written language is in fact a vocalization tool. The ancient Anglo-Saxons and Normans who invented the English language didn't have recording devices, MP3 players, or digital playback machines. To carry speech over distances longer than they could shout, they invented a system of stringing together letters and words to form speech. When you read, you almost can't help speaking the words because written English was designed to convey the sound of words on paper or parchment.

You also vocalize when you read, if you had a typical reading education, because you learned to read by vocalizing. Vocalizing is a legacy of the sound-it-out reading education you received in elementary school. You were taught oral reading skills — that letters and letter combinations make certain sounds and that you should speak these sounds as you read.

These skills are fine for beginning readers because they help beginners decode and pronounce words they see on the page. But to be a speed reader you must drop the oral reading skills you were taught and embrace silent reading skills.

Did you detect any movement or feeling in your vocal apparatus when you read this paragraph? Did you hear the words? The degree to which you heard the words or felt movement in your lips and tongue determines how much you vocalize.

Determining what type of reader you are

Reading educators distinguish between three types of vocalization. In order from most to least vocal, they are *motor readers, auditory readers,* and *visual readers.* Use the results of the vocalization test you took in the previous section to identify your reading type:

- **Motor reader:** These readers tend to move their lips and may even mimic speech with their tongues and vocal cords when reading. Their reading range is very slow (150 to 200 words per minute) because they must read word-by-word at the rate they speak. These readers have poor comprehension due to their slow reading speed.

- **Auditory reader:** These readers don't engage their lips, tongue, or vocal cords when they read, but they do silently say and hear the words. They read in the 200 to 400 words-per-minute range. Auditory readers are skillful readers with vocabularies large enough that they can quickly recognize words.

- **Visual reader:** These readers vocalize minimally or not at all. Visual readers engage their eyes and minds when they read, but not their mouths, throats, or ears. They can read many words at once because they read ideas, not individual words. They read at a rate of 400+ words per minute.

To be a speed reader, you must endeavor to be a visual reader.

Getting Away from Vocalization

Stopping yourself from vocalizing is an essential first step to becoming a speed reader. Vocalizing keeps you from reading thought unit by thought unit across the page.

If you're an auditory reader, breaking the vocalization habit is a matter of perseverance. If you're a motor reader, you have some more work to do to break the vocalization habit. Never fear, because the following sections give you tips for kicking vocalization to the curb, as well as an exercise to practice your newfound techniques.

Reading for meaning rather than sound

Reading without vocalizing has a lot in common with listening to someone speak. Imagine you're listening to a friend describe a trip to Mexico. Do you hear your friend's words, or do you hear her descriptions, thoughts, and ideas?

When someone speaks, you hear the words, but you only hear them in connection with whatever thoughts and ideas the speaker is trying to convey. The same is true of reading without vocalizing: You read words for meaning, not sound, much as you do when listening to someone speak. You see the word on the page and respond to its meaning without the intermediary step of hearing the word's sound. You don't read the words as words — you read *units of meaning* (like ideas, thoughts, and descriptions) whose building blocks happen to be words. (Head to Chapter 7 for more on units of meaning.)

Look at it this way: When you read a single word — *generous*, for example — you don't read it syllable by syllable: *gen-er-ous*. You glance at the word — *generous* — and instantly understand its meaning. Likewise when you read without vocalizing, you don't read word by word:

> He — was — generous — to — a — fault.

You read thought unit by thought unit:

> He was generous — to a fault.

This is exactly what happens when you listen to someone speak — you respond to thought units, not individual words.

Stopping the vocalization motor

To prevent your lips from moving when you read and disengage your vocal system, try putting your mouth to work at something besides reading. Chew gum, or, if your lip movements are especially pronounced, place a pencil or pen between your lips as you read.

Don't be discouraged if you have trouble understanding the words and moving from word to word on the page when you first try one of these techniques. You will be extremely uncomfortable the first few times you read with gum in your mouth or a pencil or pen between your lips. Stay with it. Most motor readers who try these strategies quickly lose the habit of moving their lips while they read.

Silencing your inner reading voice

Here are some techniques for training yourself to read without hearing your inner reading voice:

- **Try to perceive the words rather than see them.** Imagine that each word is a symbol (not a sound) that conveys a meaning.

- **Turn off your ears.** Pretend your ears have a volume control and turn it to the mute setting.

- **Widen your field of vision.** By taking in more words on a line, you force yourself to read more words at a time, and this helps prevent vocalization. Chapter 6 looks at widening your field of vision.

- **Identify the thought units in sentences, not the words, and read thought unit by thought unit rather than word by word.** Chapter 7 delves into recognizing and utilizing thought units.

- **Concentrate harder when you read.** Much of being a speed reader comes down to concentrating harder than you used to.

Exercising to quiet your inner reader

Exercise 2-1 lets you practice breaking the vocalization habit. You read the essay "The Revolutionary War" twice. First you read as you normally do, and then you read without vocalizing.

Follow these steps to complete the first half of Exercise 2-1.

1. **Note the time you start reading.**

2. **Read the first presentation of "The Revolutionary War" (Practice Text 2-1a).**

   In this reading, don't try to silence or mute your inner reading voice. Read as you normally do.

3. **After you finish reading, record your reading time on the worksheet in Appendix B.**

Practice Text 2-1a

The Revolutionary War
Courtesy of www.StrugglingReaders.com

The Revolutionary War was America's struggle for independence from England.

The dictionary defines revolution as "complete change." A revolution is an uprising by the people. It attempts to destroy

---
Practice Text 2-1a *(continued)*
---

the social or political system of a country. Then it replaces the system with a new system, often by war and bloodshed. Revolutions happen when people in a country are suffering a hardship or want changes to be made.

One of the most famous revolutions in history occurred in America in 1776. The American colonies broke away from Great Britain and became an independent republic. (Colonies are areas of land under the control of another country.) The Revolutionary War, or the American Revolution, was fought between Great Britain and its thirteen colonies that lay along the Atlantic Ocean in North America.

Tensions between Great Britain and the American colonies had been building for more than ten years before the Revolutionary War began. Great Britain and the American colonies disagreed about a number of things, especially laws, taxes, and trade regulations.

However, the Americans had become used to self rule, and they strongly resisted the new laws, especially tax laws. These laws forced them to pay money to Great Britain but wouldn't allow them any representation in the British Parliament. The Parliament is the main law-making body, made up of the King or Queen, the Lord, and the elected representatives of the people.

The colonies insisted upon "no taxation without representation." Citizens of Massachusetts were used to a representative form of government and town meetings. They believed they had a right to participate in government and should not be taxed unless represented in government.

American colonists also objected to paying taxes on British imports, goods brought in from Britain. The colonies reacted to the British taxes by banning all British imports. In what was known as the Boston Tea Party, the colonists boarded three British tea ships in Boston Harbor on December 16, 1773. They threw the cargoes overboard, fifteen thousand pounds of tea into the Boston Harbor.

The Patriots, a group of Americans who loved, defended, and supported their country, fired the first shots of the war on April 19, 1775, at Lexington, Massachusetts, and at nearby Concord. Initially the war went badly for the Americans, who were unprepared for war. The British had superior weapons and a professional military. However, the British being far from home, transporting weapons and men was difficult.

(continued)

Practice Text 2-1a *(continued)*

The colonial militias (a body of men not belonging to a regular army, but trained as soldiers to serve only in their home country) made up mostly of farmers won many encounters. But compared with the British soldiers, they were poorly trained. It was only after General Washington took charge of the Continental Army and began training the soldiers that the rebelling forces won major battles and eventually the war.

On September 3, 1783, eight years after the war began, the colonies declared their victory, and Great Britain signed the Treaty of Paris. The important document stated that the American colonies were no longer under British rule. The colonies had won their independence from Great Britain. They had become a new nation, the United States of America.

The Revolutionary War became a symbol for a new way of thinking. It was a legendary example to people in other lands who later fought to gain their freedom. American author Ralph Waldo Emerson referred to the first shot fired by the Patriots at Concord as "the shot heard around the world."

The American Revolution was the first time in history that a people fought for their independence based on principles such as rule of law, constitutional rights, and *popular sovereignty, authority belonging to the people.*

Follow these steps to complete the second half of Exercise 2-1:

1. **Note the time you start reading the second presentation of "The Revolutionary War" (Practice Text 2-1b).**

2. **Read the second presentation, as much as you're able, without hearing your inner reading voice.**

   For this presentation of the essay, to help keep you from vocalizing, I have divided the words into thought units and units of meaning. Reading the words without vocalizing at all is impossible, but do your best to suppress your inner reading voice.

3. **After you finish reading the second presentation of the essay, write down how long it took you to read it in Appendix B, and compare your first reading time to your second reading time to determine which presentation you read faster.**

Practice Text 2-1b

The Revolutionary War

The Revolutionary War was
America's struggle for
independence from England.
The dictionary defines revolution
as "complete change."
A revolution is
an uprising by the people.
It attempts to destroy
the social or political system
of a country.
Then it replaces the system
with a new system,
often by war and bloodshed.
Revolutions happen when people
in a country
are suffering a hardship
or want changes to be made.
One of the most famous revolutions
in history occurred
in America in 1776.
The American colonies broke away
from Great Britain and
became an independent republic.
(Colonies are areas of land
under the control
of another country.)
The Revolutionary War,
or the American Revolution,
was fought between Great Britain
and its thirteen colonies

that lay along the Atlantic Ocean
in North America.
Tensions between Great Britain
and the American colonies
had been building
for more than ten years
before the Revolutionary War began.
Great Britain and the American colonies
disagreed about a number of things,
especially laws, taxes,
and trade regulations.
However, the Americans had become
used to self rule,
and they strongly resisted
the new laws,
especially tax laws.
These laws forced them
to pay money to Great Britain
but wouldn't allow them
any representation
in the British Parliament.
The Parliament is the main
law-making body,
made up of the King or Queen,
the Lord, and
the elected representatives of the people.
The colonies insisted upon
"no taxation without representation."
Citizens of Massachusetts

(continued)

Practice Text 2-1b *(continued)*

were used to a representative
form of government and town meetings
and believed they had a right
to participate in government.
They should not be taxed
unless represented in government.
American colonists also objected
to paying taxes on British imports,
goods brought in from Britain.
The colonies reacted to the British taxes
by banning all British imports.
In what was known as
the Boston Tea Party,
the colonists boarded
three British tea ships
in Boston Harbor on December 16, 1773.
They threw the cargoes overboard,
fifteen thousand pounds of tea
into the Boston Harbor.
The Patriots, a group of Americans
who loved, defended, and supported their country,
fired the first shots of the war
on April 19, 1775, at Lexington, Massachusetts,
and at nearby Concord.
Initially the war went badly
for the Americans,
who were unprepared for war.
The British had superior weapons
and a professional military.
However, the British being far from home,
transporting weapons and men was difficult.

The colonial militias
(a body of men not belonging
to a regular army,
but trained as soldiers
to serve only in their home country)
made up mostly of farmers
won many encounters.
But compared with the British soldiers,
they were poorly trained.
It was only after General Washington
took charge of the Continental Army
and began training the soldiers
that the rebelling forces
won major battles
and eventually the war.
On September 3, 1783,
eight years after the war began,
the colonies declared their victory,
and Great Britain signed the Treaty of Paris.
The important document stated
that the American colonies were
no longer under British rule.
The colonies had won their independence
from Great Britain.
They had become a new nation,
the United States of America.
The Revolutionary War became
a symbol for a new way of thinking.
It was a legendary example
to people in other lands
who later fought to gain their freedom.

Practice Text 2-1b *(continued)*

American author Ralph Waldo Emerson that a people fought for

referred to the first shot fired their independence based on

by the Patriots at Concord principles such as rule of law,

as "the shot heard around the world." constitutional rights,

The American Revolution *and popular sovereignty,*

was the first time in history authority belonging to the people.

 You probably read the second presentation faster. By quieting your inner reading voice, by taking in several words at a time, you can really pick up your reading speed.

Preventing Regression When You Read

Reading educators use the term *regression* to describe the act of moving your eyes backward to reread words and sentences you've already read. You regress if you lose confidence in understanding what you've read and believe you have to go back.

Sometimes regressing is necessary. If you're reading a dry technical manual or academic paper, you can't help but regress (or yawn) from time to time. Sometimes regressing is the author's fault. Reading is a collaboration between the author and reader, but if the author doesn't live up to his side of the bargain (if he writes badly), you have to regress to material you've already read to figure out what the heck is going on.

Obviously, regression slows your reading speed. It takes twice as long to turn back and read what you've already read. Worse, regression also slows comprehension because you lose the flow of meaning in the words. For example, consider these two paragraphs. In the first, you read without regressing. The second paragraph demonstrates what readers read when they regress:

> The steeplechase is a kind of distance horse race in which horse and rider jump fences, jump ditches, and face other obstacles. The races originated in Ireland in the 18th century. The race gets its name because originally the contestants raced from the church steeple in one town to the church steeple in another.

The steeplechase is a kind of distance horse race in which horse and — distance horse race — rider jump fences, jump ditches, and face other obstacles — jump fences, jump ditches. The races originated in Ireland in the 18th century. The race gets its name — 18th century — because originally the contestants raced — gets its name — from the church steeple in one town to the church steeple in another.

The second paragraph is a jumbled mess, but it's what readers see when they regress in the course of reading. It's what they comprehend, too, if they comprehend anything at all.

If you compulsively regress in your reading, you can do something about it. Resist the urge to regress by forcing yourself to do the opposite of what it tells you to do. Forge ahead in your reading. Eventually, you lose the compulsion to regress and start to understand that regressing isn't as necessary as you thought it was for understanding what you read.

If regressing is an especially thorny problem for you, try this technique to keep yourself from regressing. Get an index card or fold a piece of paper that's as long as the line of text you're reading. As you finish reading each line, cover it with the card or paper. This way, you can't see earlier lines and you can't regress.

But I regress. . .

Here are some other reasons readers regress:

- ✔ **They vocalize.** As I explain earlier in this chapter, vocalization occurs when you hear the words as you read them. When you vocalize, your eyes race ahead of your mouth as you read, and you get confused when the disparity between what your inner reading voice says and what your eyes see becomes too great. You have to return to material you already read to make sure you read it correctly.

- ✔ **They're compelled to.** Some people regress for the same reason that they double- and triple-check to make sure their car keys are in their pocket or purse — they're compulsive about it. They don't trust their ability to understand what they read, so they reread material again and again.

- ✔ **They believe the slower-is-better myth.** Some people regress because they believe in the myth that the only way to get good comprehension is to read slowly, purposefully, and repetitively. As I argue in Chapter 1 of this book, speed reading actually increases comprehension.

Chapter 3

Understanding the Mechanics of Speed Reading

*W*ith the goal of improving your speed-reading mechanics so that you can apply them to the speed-reading skills in Chapter 4, this chapter explains what happens in your eyes and mind when you speed read. It explains what eye fixations are, what your vision span is, and how you can increase your reading speed by widening your reading vision. This chapter also looks into how you comprehend when you read and how to choose reading strategies when you begin reading a new book, article, or Web page.

Fixating on Eye Fixations

For your eyes to see anything, they have to be still. You can't swing your eyes wildly around the room and expect to see anything but a blur. To see anything clearly — your fingernail, a bug on the window sill, the neighbor's yard, the highest peak on the horizon, a star in the sky — your eyes must be still.

The same is true of reading words on a page. To see words, your eyes must be still, but they must also move left-to-right across the page to take in words in the act of reading.

How can your eyes be still and move at the same time? The answer is *eye fixations*. When you read, your eyes move in fits and starts across the page. They fixate on an individual word or a group of words and then move along to the next word or word group when you have comprehended the first one. In this way, you read across each line of text.

Looking at eye fixations

For many years, researchers took for granted the idea that everybody reads one word at a time. They believed that fast readers were simply people who could identify and comprehend individual words quickly, one after the next.

Starting about 1910, however, researchers interested in improving students' reading abilities conducted experiments to see precisely what happens when you read. They discovered eye fixations. They noticed that the eyes do not move at a steady rate across the page but rather by fits and starts. They also discovered that the fewer eye fixations you have when reading, the faster you read. This breakthrough discovery was the beginning of modern speed reading.

Figure 3-1 demonstrates a single eye fixation. The eyes are focused on the fixation point, but they can see letters and words to the left and right of this point in the vision span. In the figure, the reader is reading three words — "in temperate regions" — in a single eye fixation.

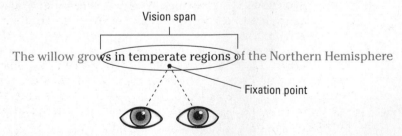

Figure 3-1: Reading three words in a single eye fixation.

You can conduct your own experiment to see how eye fixations work by following these steps:

1. **Recruit a friend who doesn't mind letting you watch him or her read.**

   If a friend isn't handy, put on a pair of dark glasses and go to a public place such as a library or waiting room where a number of people are reading.

2. **Give your friend a book or magazine article to read and observe his or her eyes in the act of reading.**

   If you're watching a stranger read, be discreet. Make sure your dark glasses are riding high on your nose; better yet, put on a pair of Groucho glasses.

3. **Notice how the reader's eyes move.**

   They remain for a fraction of a second in one place and then jerk to the right, where they remain for another fraction of a second and jerk to the right again. What you see are eye fixations. After arriving at the end of the line, the eyes sweep to the left and fixate on a position at the start of the next line, and the eye fixations begin anew.

4. **To count how many eye fixations occur on a line, ask the reader to tell you when he or she comes to the end of each line. You better skip this step if you're watching a stranger read.)**

   Some lines of text require more eye fixations to read than others, depending on a number of factors including how long the line is, how familiar the reader is with the topic, and whether the words in the line are in the reader's vocabulary.

As well as seeing the subject's eyes jerk to the right, you may see them jerk to the left. Eyes fixate right to left when the reader regresses in the act of reading. As Chapter 2 explains, *regression* occurs when you move backward to reread text and make sure you understood it correctly.

Eye fixations and reading speed

Readers who make fewer eye fixations read faster because they take in more words with each fixation. Instead of taking in 1 or 2 words at a time, fast readers can see and process 3 to 14 words in a single eye fixation.

The number of words you can process in an eye fixation depends on your vision span, your vocabulary, and your familiarity with what you're reading, which I cover in the following sections.

Eye fixations and your vision span

The wider your vision span is, the more words you can process in an eye fixation and the faster you can read. Acquiring the ability to see many words at a time is essential for speed reading. To see why, consider this sentence:

The rain in Spain falls mainly on the plain.

A slow reader with a narrow vision span reads this sentence slowly in six to nine eye fixations, sometimes taking in only a single word per fixation. This reader has to work harder to comprehend the sentence because the meaning of the words arrives disconnectedly in short bursts. In the following version of the sentence, I inserted slashes to represent where a slow reader would fixate her eyes in the course of reading:

The rain \ in Spain \ falls \ mainly \ on \ the plain.

A fast reader with a wider vision span can read the sentence in two or three eye fixations. This reader has a stronger comprehension because she reads the sentence phrase by phrase (or thought unit by thought unit — more on this terminology in Chapter 7), and phrases convey more meaning than individual words. In this version of the sentence, I added slashes to represent where a fast reader would fixate his or her eyes in the course of reading. The fast reader reads the sentence in only two eye fixations:

The rain in Spain falls \ mainly on the plain.

Eye fixations and your vocabulary

To see how eye fixations correlate to vocabulary, read these lines carefully and try to understand their meaning:

Sownynge in moral vertu was his speche,

And gladly wolde he lerne, and gladly teche.

Unless you understand Middle English or you're familiar with the writings of Geoffrey Chaucer (these lines come from *The Canterbury Tales*), you had trouble with these lines because few of the words are in your vocabulary. You didn't recognize the words, so you had to examine them one at a time and probably read the lines in 15 (or more) eye fixations, one for each word.

Reading this translation of Chaucer's lines is considerably easier because all or most of the words are in your vocabulary. Notice how much faster you read the translation:

Filled with moral virtue was his speech,

And gladly would he learn, and gladly teach.

You read the translation faster because you needed fewer eye fixations to read it. You probably read the translation in eight or fewer fixations. Because the words were familiar, you didn't have to dwell on them, and you could read more than one word at a time.

 The larger your vocabulary is, the more words you recognize off the bat when you read. You can take in more words with an eye fixation when you recognize the words, which is why enlarging your vocabulary is essential to being a speed reader. Check out Chapter 12 for more on expanding your vocabulary.

Eye fixations and topic familiarity

How familiar you are with a topic is another factor influencing how many words you can see in a single eye fixation. When you read about a topic in your area of expertise or field of interest, you read more confidently, and you're able to read more quickly with fewer eye fixations because you're at home with the author's words and terminology.

Your background, your general knowledge, your knowledge base (to borrow a computer term), your education — these factors also determine how fast you can read. People with a breadth of knowledge read faster because more is familiar to them. By making reading more efficient and pleasurable, speed reading encourages you to read, which in turn widens your breadth of knowledge and makes you read even faster.

Exercising Your Eye Fixations

Exercise 3-1 is designed to help you understand where your eyes fixate when you read and the role eye fixations play in reading. In Practice Text 3-1, you see two side-by-side versions of an essay called "Say Thanks Before It's Just a Memory" by nationally syndicated columnist Harvey Mackay (originally published October 4, 1998). Follow these steps to complete the exercise:

1. **Note the time you start reading.**

2. **Read the essay on the left at your normal reading speed**.

   The number to the right of each line tells you how many words are in that line.

3. **After you finish reading, write down how long it took to read the first version of essay on the worksheet in Appendix B.**

4. **Note the time you start reading the second presentation of the essay, the one on the right side of the page.**

5. **Read the essay and try to fixate on each line the number of recommended times.**

   To the left of each line in this essay is a number that tells you how many times to fixate your eyes in that line. To help with your eye fixations, I've italicized every other set of words that I want you to fixate on. Try to limit the number of times you fixate on each line to the number indicated.

6. **After you finish reading the second presentation of the essay, write down how long you take to read it in Appendix B and compare your first reading time to your second reading time.**

   Did you read faster when you made fewer eye fixations?

Practice Text 3-1

Fixations at each word	# of fixations	Fixation/several per line
Text presented in normal format		Text presented in normal format with suggested eye fixations identified
Say Thanks Before It's Just a Memory **By Harvey Mackay**		**Say Thanks Before It's Just a Memory** **By Harvey Mackay**
Some time ago the owner of a small but profitable	10 vs. 3	*Some time ago the owner of a small but profitable*
business wrote columnist Ann Landers about his	7 vs. 3	*business wrote columnist Ann Landers about his*
practice of giving annual bonuses to his employees.	7 vs. 3	*practice of giving annual bonuses to his employees.*
The amounts were based on time served and salary	7 vs. 2	*The amounts were based on time served and salary*
levels.	4 vs. 1	*levels.*
He had been doing it for 16 years and in all that	12 vs. 3	*He had been doing it for 16 years and in all that*
time only two employees had ever said "thank	8 vs. 3	*time only two employees had ever said "thank*
you." Neither were still with the company. One	8 vs. 3	*you." Neither were still with the company. One*
passed away, and the other took early retirement.	8 vs. 2	*passed away, and the other took early retirement.*
The owner vowed that he wasn't going to give any	10 vs. 3	*The owner vowed that he wasn't going to give any*
more bonuses, and if anyone complained, the	7 vs. 2	*more bonuses, and if anyone complained, the*
response would be "There will be no bonuses this	9 vs. 2	*response would be "There will be no bonuses this*
year because not one of our current employees has	9 vs. 2	*year because not one of our current employees has*
taken the time and trouble to say 'thank you.'"	9 vs. 3	*taken the time and trouble to say 'thank you.'"*
In her answer, Ann Landers segued from that letter	9 vs. 3	*In her answer, Ann Landers segued from that letter*
to the tons of letters she receives from others,	9 vs. 2	*to the tons of letters she receives from others,*

(continued)

Practice Text 3-1 *(continued)*

parents and grandparents particularly, who want to know what to do about gifts that are not acknowledged. What happened? Did the poor thing lose the power of speech or the use of their writing hand? Did they fall off the ends of the earth? Was the gift lost in the mail?	7 vs. 2 8 vs. 2 7 vs. 2 11 vs. 2 11 vs. 2 5 vs. 2	parents and grandparents particularly, *who want to know* what to do about gifts *that are not acknowledged.* What happened? *Did the poor thing* lose the power of speech or the use *of their writing hand?* Did they fall off *the ends of the earth?* Was the gift *lost in the mail?*
How many times have we sent a birthday check and not heard a word back, the only evidence that the gift was received and found among the pile of canceled checks returned from the bank?	10 vs. 3 1 vs. 0 11 vs. 2 7 vs. 2	How many times *have we sent a birthday check* and not heard a word back, *the only evidence that* the gift was received and *found among the pile of* canceled checks *returned from the bank?*
How many times have you given a larger than normal tip without any recognition? Waiters and waitresses should realize a larger tip is a signal that a customer enjoyed the experience and wants to return, particularly if their generosity is acknowledged. Diners even have been known to ask for a favorite waitperson's station.	9 vs. 2 7 vs. 2 10 vs. 3 8 vs. 2 6 vs. 3 7 vs. 1 6 vs. 2	How many times *have you given* a larger than normal tip *without any recognition?* Waiters and waitresses should realize a *larger tip is a signal that* a customer enjoyed the experience *and wants to* return, particularly *if their generosity is* acknowledged. *Diners even have been known to* ask for a favorite *waitperson's station.*
If you're a salesperson or own a company and have recently received a larger than expected order from a customer, what have you done to make that customer know how you feel about it? It's great to	10 vs. 3 8 vs. 2 9 vs. 3 10 vs. 2	*If you're a salesperson* or own a company *and have* recently received a larger than expected order *from a customer,* what have you done to *make that* customer know how you feel about it? *It's great to*

Practice Text 3-1 *(continued)*

take your spouse out to dinner to celebrate your great sales ability, but what about the guy or gal who gave you the order?	9 vs. 2 10 vs. 1 5 vs. 1	*take your spouse out to dinner to celebrate your great sales ability, but what about the guy or gal who gave you the order?*
A thank you is just good manners. A prompt thank you is easy to say, a lot easier to say than "Gee, I forgot to tell you how much I appreciated your order," or "How've you been after all this time?"	10 vs. 3 13 vs. 3 9 vs. 1 9 vs. 2	*A thank you is just good manners. A prompt thank you is easy to say, a lot easier to say than "Gee, I forgot to tell you how much I appreciated your order," or "How've you been after all this time?"*
In New York City, the police are enforcing the quality-of-life laws and Mayor Giuliani is even calling for New York City's cabdrivers and waiters to improve their manners, pointing out that rudeness is not a great civic selling point. It seems to be working. Crime is down. Tourism is up. New York City is on a roll.	9 vs. 2 9 vs. 3 8 vs. 2 7 vs. 2 10 vs. 3 10 vs. 2 6 vs. 1	*In New York City, the police are enforcing the quality-of-life laws and Mayor Giuliani is even calling for New York City's cabdrivers and waiters to improve their manners, pointing out that rudeness is not a great civic selling point. It seems to be working. Crime is down. Tourism is up. New York City is on a roll.*
Many companies wait until the holidays to say thank you. There's nothing the matter with that, but why wait? It's a lot more personal and responsive to seize the day and say the magic words the moment it's appropriate. And forget the stuff with your corporate logo on it as a thank you. It's fine as advertising. For yourself. But it isn't a gift.	8 vs. 3 9 vs. 2 9 vs. 2 10 vs. 2 8 vs. 2 12 vs. 2 8 vs. 2	*Many companies wait until the holidays to say thank you. There's nothing the matter with that, but why wait? It's a lot more personal and responsive to seize the day and say the magic words the moment it's appropriate. And forget the stuff with your corporate logo on it as a thank you. It's fine as advertising. For yourself. But it isn't a gift.*

(continued)

Practice Text 3-1 (continued)

The best gifts I have ever received have no monetary value but what I call momento value. They are the letters I receive from people who have used tips or advice I've given in speeches, columns or books to get jobs, bonuses or unexpected orders.	9 vs. 3 8 vs. 2 10 vs. 3 9 vs. 2 9 vs. 3	*The best gifts I have ever received have no monetary value but what I call momento value. They are the letters I receive from people who have used tips or advice I've given in speeches, columns or books to get jobs, bonuses or unexpected orders.*
When a 72-year-old woman wrote to thank me for helping her make a dynamic splash in her chosen field, I was on cloud nine for days. And what an upper it was to hear from a man in prison that he'd begun to turn his life around thanks to the inspiration he'd received from one of my books.	11 vs. 2 9 vs. 3 11 vs. 2 12 vs. 3 9 vs. 2 8 vs. 2	*When a 72-year-old woman wrote to thank me for helping her make a dynamic splash in her chosen field, I was on cloud nine for days. And what an upper it was to hear from a man in prison that he'd begun to turn his life around thanks to the inspiration he'd received from one of my books.*
One area of thank-you territory that many of us neglect is our formative years. They don't call them "formative" for nothing. Have you ever said thanks to the teachers and coaches that lifted you up, dusted you off and set you straight when you were trying to figure out what growing up was all about? Believe me, a note or even a phone call from you would be well received.	10 vs. 2 9 vs. 2 8 vs. 2 9 vs. 2 10 vs. 3 10 vs. 2 11 vs. 3 4 vs. 1	*One area of thank-you territory that many of us neglect is our formative years. They don't call them "formative" for nothing. Have you ever said thanks to the teachers and coaches that lifted you up, dusted you off and set you straight when you were trying to figure out what growing up was all about? Believe me, a note or even a phone call from you would be well received.*

Comprehending Comprehension Mechanics

One reason a speed reader comprehends better than a slow reader is the speed reader's superior ability to absorb the author's thoughts and ideas in into his or her short-term memory. When you read slowly, you actually confuse your short-term memory, and this confusion impairs your ability to understand what you're reading. The following sections explain how speed reading helps you exploit your short-term memory to better understand what you read.

Reading and your short-term memory

The short-term memory is a part of your brain that initially absorbs information. It can hold no more than five to seven facts or concepts, and only for a short period of time (which is why you forget that seven-digit phone number you just looked up if someone interrupts you before you can dial). After that initial short-term storage period, the facts are either crowded out by other facts or assimilated into your long-term memory, where they become a part of your permanent knowledge.

Reading is the act of assimilating information, first into your short-term memory, and then (if you're able to assimilate it further) into your long-term memory. Here is roughly what happens when you read:

1. In a single eye fixation, you take in 1 to 14 words.

2. Your eyes move along the sentence to another fixation point. During this fraction of a second, an image of the words you saw flashes to your brain and is stored as a *unit of meaning* in your short-term memory.

3. Your mind calls for more units of meaning.

4. You take in another 1 to 14 words in an eye fixation.

5. Your eyes again move along the sentence, and an image of the last unit of meaning you took in flashes in your brain. This unit enters your short-term memory beside the unit of meaning that is already there.

These steps are repeated until your short-term memory fills to capacity. At that time, concepts you have imported into your short-term memory either disappear or are recoded (chunked) so that your long-term memory can retain them.

Assimilating concepts and ideas

Cognitive psychologists use the term *chunking* to describe how your brain reorganizes concepts and ideas you've absorbed in your short-term memory and applies them to your own experience so you can understand them. Chunking is essentially what happens when you retain what you've read.

Speed readers are better chunkers — they comprehend reading material better — because they can hold more advanced concepts in their short-term memories. Rather than five to seven words or small word groups, they can hold five to seven complex thought units. When the time comes to absorb the information and make it their own, they have more material to work with. More of the author's ideas come to them at once.

For example, consider how a slow and a fast reader take in this paragraph differently:

> The rotator cuff is a group of four muscles (and their tendons) that stabilize and govern movement of the shoulder. The muscles form a covering around the top of the upper arm bone (humerus). The rotator cuff enables the arm to rotate.

A slow reader with a narrow vision span can only hold a few of these concepts at once in short-term memory: rotator cuff, muscle group, four muscles with tendons, stability, movement. But a fast reader capable of reading many words at the same time can take in the entire paragraph in five to seven eye fixations. A fast reader can take in and assimilate the whole of the author's ideas.

Exploring the Pacer Question

The stereotypical speed reader reads with a pacer. A *pacer* is a visual aid — it can be your finger, your hand, or a paper pacer — that assists in speed reading. In the stereotype, the speed reader runs his finger down the page, frantically gobbling words at a hundred miles per hour and absorbing an entire page almost as fast as he can turn the page.

Many speed-reading courses include instructions for using your finger or hand as a pacer when you read. You learn the relative merits of different pacer motions (such as the Vulcan, the Open-Hand Wiggle, and the Snake) and when to use this or that pacer motion in your reading.

Here's my take on using a pacer: A pacer can be helpful when you're a beginning speed reader, but you should abandon the pacer as soon as you grasp the fundamentals of speed reading.

I suggest using a pacer, which can help you to focus on word clumps, word groups, thought units, and units of meaning as you read exercises. They help you grasp more than one word at a time in your reading and expand your vision so you can take in several words at a time.

Similarly, using your hand or forefinger as a pacer can help you expand your vision. Moving your hand or finger down the page encourages you to expand your vertical vision and see words on more than one line. If you want to experiment with using your hand or finger as a pacer, I'm not going to stop you. Check it out and see if works for you. If you want to use your mouse cursor as a pacer when you read on your computer screen, I'm not going to stop you there either. It may be helpful.

However, I believe that pacers in the long run don't enable you to read faster, and I'm not alone. Many reading educators believe that using a pacer can be detrimental to reading speed and comprehension. You read with your eyes and your brain, not your fingers. The mental resources you apply to moving your finger on the page can be put to better use expanding your vision and recognizing word groups and thought units with your eyes and brain. After you have mastered the fundamentals of speed reading, using a pacer is a distraction. It actually slows down your reading.

The mother of invention

Evelyn Wood, the speed reading pioneer, popularized the use of pacers in speed reading. Wood's speed reading courses were advertised on television in the 1960, 1970s, and 1980s; she coined the term *speed reading*. I knew Evelyn, and she once told me how she got the idea to use pacers: Frustrated that she couldn't read faster, she threw the book she was reading on the ground. When she brushed the dirt off its pages, she discovered the usefulness of moving her hand down the page to increase her reading speed.

Deciding How Much to Bring to Your Reading

Before you start reading anything, ask yourself, "How much do I need to bring to my reading?"

How fast you read and the level of concentration you bring to your reading is really a question of why you read. If you're reading for pleasure, read slowly and luxuriate in the words. If time is of the essence because you're reading for an exam or important meeting, you have no choice but to read quickly.

Here are some questions to ask yourself before you decide how much to bring to what you read.

- ✔ **How important is retaining the knowledge I get from this reading?** For example, if you're exploring a topic that will advance your career, you need to read with care. For that matter, you may consider underlining words or writing notes in the margin. This type of reading requires your utmost concentration. On the other hand, if you're reading a menu, you can read entirely at your leisure.

- ✔ **What do I want to get out of this reading?** How you answer this question determines how fast you read. If your reading has an important purpose — if you will be tested on what you read or you need the information for a paper or presentation — you must read with a higher level of concentration. But if you're reading the sports pages of the newspaper or a detective novel, you can take your sweet time.

- ✔ **What type of information is being presented?** Facts and figures require more concentration to absorb. On the other hand, dialogue is easy to read.

Chapter 4

Introducing Speed-Reading Fundamentals

....

In This Chapter

▶ Expanding your horizontal and vertical vision span

▶ Reading word by word and clump by clump

▶ Testing your ability to recognize and read word groups

▶ Developing the mindset of a speed reader

....

This chapter takes you on a tour of speed-reading fundamentals; along the way, you get the opportunity to do speed-reading exercises. The idea is for you to see for yourself why grasping the fundamentals of speed reading can vastly improve your speed-reading skills.

By applying yourself to the speed-reading exercises in this chapter — by doing each exercise — you can become a better, more aware speed reader. Although completing all the exercises obviously gives you the greatest benefit, even taking on just a couple of them shows you how easily speed reading improves your reading.

Remember: The concepts introduced in this chapter are explained in more detail throughout this book. I just want you to get your feet wet here. Don't be shy. The water isn't that cold.

Widening Your Vision Span

As Chapter 3 explains in detail, your eyes move across the page in stops and starts called *eye fixations,* and with each fixation, they settle on one word or set of words after another. To improve your reading speed, you need to take in more words with each eye fixation, and to do that, you need to increase your *vision span.*

Exercise 4-1 makes you aware of how your eyes move — that is, your eye fixations — when you read and gives you practice in widening your vision span. The exercise presents four-, five-, six-, and seven-digit numbers; the goal is for you to read and process each number in a single eye fixation.

For this exercise, you need a pen or pencil and a piece of paper to write on, plus a pacer. This exercise tests and strengthens your ability to see many characters at once. Follow these instructions to complete the exercise:

1. **Moving your pacer down the first column of Practice Text 4-1, glance at a number.**

   Only look at the number one time. Don't linger — see whether you can take it in with one glance.

2. **Write down the number on your piece of paper.**

3. **Repeat Steps 1 and 2 until you've moved your pacer down all the columns and written down all the numbers.**

4. **Compare the numbers you wrote down to the actual numbers and record your correct/incorrect scores on the worksheet in Appendix B.**

Chances are you wrote down a few numbers incorrectly, but that's okay. As you become more aware of your eye fixations when you read, your vision span will widen, and you'll become more adept at reading more digits and numbers with a single eye fixation. After you have more experience with speed reading, retry this exercise and see whether your score improves.

Practice Text 4-1

4032	23449	129848	4611453
4146	25158	293729	2353397
4942	22183	359413	4174954
1070	29576	395897	4884978
1508	15684	499766	1880107
4733	42616	446741	1036566
4464	31064	214520	1077561
1664	30398	291505	3583188
4335	27886	209902	2645073

Practice Text 4-1 *(continued)*

3137	15480	435698	4886190
2673	34812	263367	1581101
1379	15953	288432	1224516
3759	48029	353239	3959503
4597	20754	475738	4432688
4795	37213	177659	3727465
3322	46792	263020	4623933
2362	19832	110655	1232459
3859	37925	375807	1274676
1836	13585	189272	4628069
2089	37603	293609	4809881

Exercise 4-2 also helps you widen your horizontal vision span. For this exercise, you need a pen or pencil and a pacer. Follow these steps:

1. **Choose a target number (a number from 1 to 9).**

2. **Move the pacer to the first line of Practice Text 4-2, direct your eyes at the middle number (it's italicized to help you identify it), and read the numbers on that line.**

   Try to take in all the numbers in the line in a single glance. Don't move your eyes left or right from that italicized number.

3. **Notice how many times the target number you chose in Step 1 appears in the row of numbers.**

   For example, if you choose *3* as your target number, notice in the first line that the number *3* appears twice.

4. **At the end of the line, write down how many times the target number appears without glancing back at the numbers.**

   If your target number appears twice, for example, write *2* at the end of the line.

5. **Move the pacer down the lines and repeat Steps 2 through 4 until you finish reading line 20.**

6. **Total the number of times your target number appeared and compare your totals to the answer key.**

   For example, if you chose *3*, your target number appeared 20 times.

   Repeat this exercise five or six times, choosing a different target number each time. Your ability to pick out target numbers will increase as you repeat the exercise.

Practice Text 4-2

1	4	1	4	4	6	3	1	3	4
2	2	4	2	7	5	6	9	1	2
3	1	2	6	6	2	6	2	6	2
4	3	3	4	2	6	9	5	4	2
5	6	9	3	1	1	3	9	6	8
6	5	9	3	5	6	9	5	4	4
7	5	1	4	2	9	1	6	9	3
8	5	4	5	6	3	9	4	6	9
9	2	6	7	2	3	2	6	1	6
10	8	4	6	3	4	7	1	2	7
11	2	3	6	8	5	5	6	7	2
12	7	9	2	5	9	1	9	6	7
13	4	6	8	9	3	6	5	8	4
14	3	2	4	1	8	5	1	8	2
15	5	8	8	9	4	3	4	4	8
16	6	4	8	8	2	2	5	7	4
17	1	1	5	1	7	5	3	8	4
18	4	3	2	5	5	6	1	8	5
19	2	2	2	3	7	8	2	1	5
20	4	3	9	3	3	9	9	1	7

Answer key: Target number appears *x* times: **1:** 17; **2:** 26; **3:** 20; **4:** 28; **5:** 19; **6:** 30; **7:** 11; **8:** 14; **9:** 19.

Reading Clump by Clump

As I explain in Chapter 6, something magical happens when you stop reading word by word and start reading in clumps — you read several words with each eye fixation. Because you take in more words at a time, you don't have to decode each word as you read it. You can understand the words in context, which increases your comprehension and retention.

To help illustrate this change, check out Exercise 4-3. It presents two-, three-, and four-word phrases that carry meaning. For that reason, you can read each phrase in a single eye fixation without having to consider individual words. Your increased reading speed in this exercise demonstrates that you can read more than one word at once and that reading more than one word at time indeed increases your reading speed.

For Exercise 4-3, time how long it takes to read all the phrases in Practice Text 4-3. Using a pacer, read each phrase in one glance if you can. Write down how long this exercise takes you on the work-sheet in Appendix B.

Practice Text 4-3

Random Phrases 2 Words	Random Phrases 3 Words	Random Phrases 4 Words
years ahead	ride your bike	everyone has high expectations
accountable situation	reading a book	taking failure into account
different idea	some different ideas	continued progress is expected
favorite color	taking a hike	see to the problem
historic home	up and around	birds in the forest
eastern coast	quarterly business report	center of the town
feeling fit	hot summer days	as time goes by
hair dryer	only a year	people have different opinions
general background	hit and run	furnished house for sale
acceptable conditions	letters from friends	head for the hills
changing color	setting the standard	colors in the rainbow
character actor	climbing the hill	nothing succeeds like success

(continued)

Practice Text 4-3 *(continued)*		
Random Phrases 2 Words	Random Phrases 3 Words	Random Phrases 4 Words
dark nights	cross the grain	just around the corner
inactive account	ready for anything	having a good time
complete objection	now and then	speaking with more sincerity
daily business	an influential friend	skiing on the mountain
early morning	singing a song	painting in the gallery
drinking water	early morning clouds	planning for the future
basketball music	the flower garden	do yourself a favor
happy day	last summer day	appearances can be wrong
golden moment	nice and thin	down on the farm
hillside farm	horse and rider	animals on the farm
car parts	sooner or later	once upon a time
glass ring	people have opinions	rooms with a view

Reading Vertically as Well as Horizontally

As Chapter 6 explains, speed reading isn't just about widening your horizontal vision — it's also about being able to read words vertically on the page. Besides reading words that are side by side, you take in words that are above and below one another.

To help you get a jump on this skill, Exercise 4-4 presents two-, four-, six-, and eight-word clumps. The clumps are presented, respectively, on two, two, three, and four lines. The goal is for you to develop the ability to read words vertically on the page as well as horizontally. Don't worry — it isn't as hard as it seems.

To increase your vertical reading span, move your pacer down the columns in Practice Text 4-4, reading the word clumps as you go along. Try to take in each clump of words in a single eye fixation without *vocalizing* (saying and hearing the words as you read); vocalizing prevents you from being able to read all the words at once.

Practice Text 4-4

Random Phrases 3 Words, 2 Lines	Random Phrases 4 Words, 2 Lines	Random Phrases 6 Words, 3 Lines	Random Phrases 8 Words, 4 Lines
gold and silver	more than you know	open the window for fresher air	late arrivals are always welcome at the meetings
are suppliers ready	explore opportunities for success	very cold mornings during the winter	every company usually has a basic business plan
here and now	gone with the wind	affecting almost everyone in the neighborhood	most residents of the village seem quite friendly
around the corner	middle of the day	earthquakes happen enough around the world	substantial progress has been made for the project
are systems ready	doing business as usual	changing ideas lead to different directions	one purpose is to help raise planet awareness
singing a song	taking care of business	nothing succeeds like success in business	
forming great friendships	history in the making	showing a willingness to help others	
an active account	reading a good book		
form good friendships	command of the town		

(continued)

Practice Text 4-4 (continued)

Random Phrases 3 Words, 2 Lines	Random Phrases 4 Words, 2 Lines	Random Phrases 6 Words, 3 Lines	Random Phrases 8 Words, 4 Lines
very soft music	furnished house for sale	nothing succeeds like success in life	all appointments are scheduled on a regular basis
reading a book	writing a private letter	paintings of major artists are invaluable	one can only hope for the very best
plan of action	hoping for good things	ten miles to the next town	many good questions from the audience were answered
now and then	walking down the steps	basic business plan for the church	are there reasons for doing the right thing
based on facts	fishing in the lake	schools are invaluable in every community	nearly everyone in town supports the baseball team
explore your opportunities	ability always does count	secrets are meant to be kept	
many happy returns	early in the morning	authorize almost everyone in the neighborhood	
ready or not	head for the hills		
each election return	sending letters to families		

Practice Text 4-4 *(continued)*

Random Phrases 3 Words, 2 Lines	Random Phrases 4 Words, 2 Lines	Random Phrases 6 Words, 3 Lines	Random Phrases 8 Words, 4 Lines
the business report	everybody has common concerns	the winds blow across the pastures	looking at the stars in the night sky
visiting great friends	cold mornings in winter	nearly everybody will celebrate the occasion	taking a walk down the long dusty path
flying in formation	running in the race	most people have their own opinions	a cruise around the world would be inviting
play tennis indoors	let sleeping dogs lie	what a day this has been	major council decisions are announced by the mayor
somehow it works	members of the council	be ready to explore every opportunity	one can always hope for the very best
anyone can play	looking through the window	reservations for a very special dinner	
oil and gas	animals on the farm	everyone has an ability to succeed	
form great friendships	librarians knew about books		
walk on water	better sooner than later		

(continued)

Working with Word Groups

After you master reading clumps, you can graduate to reading word groups. As Chapter 7 explains, a *word group* is similar to a clump, except a word group has meaning — it's a collection of words that hang together in a sentence. For example, prepositional phrases and subordinate clauses are word groups. If you can spot these word groups in the course of your reading, you can read that much more quickly because you can rapidly take in the word groups.

Grasping word groups as you read

If picking up on word groups seems difficult to you, check out Exercise 4-5, which demonstrates that you already have an aptitude for perceiving word groups. In this exercise, you take in groups of words that have been scrambled and see whether you can recode them as word groups.

Practice Text 4-5 presents three- and four-word phrases. Each phrase is presented first with the words out of order and then with the words in the correct order. For this exercise, move a pacer down the column and read, in a single glance, each set of out-of-order words. As you read each set, see whether you can recode the words in the correct order and then move the pacer down the column to check your arrangement. This exercise demonstrates that you're capable of reading word groups because it shows you that you can quickly take in words without regard to their proper order.

Practice Text 4-5

Random Phrases 3 Words Out of Sequence	Random Phrases 3 Words In Sequence	Random Phrases 4 Words Out of Sequence	Random Phrases 4 Words In Sequence
differences expected are	differences are expected	there's story a great	there's a great story
him listen to	listen to him	sand desert in the	sand in the desert
hope continue to	continue to hope	video movies available on	movies available on video
production increasing is	production is increasing	on all flights time	all flights on time
deserts dry are	deserts are dry	welcome meetings at the	welcome at the meetings
for provisions travel	provisions for travel	town popularity voters among	popularity among town voters
right thing the	the right thing	in success your field	success in your field
game the watch	watch the game	printed decisions are council	council decisions are printed
in sculptures museums	sculptures in museums	corporate expected decisions are	corporate decisions are expected

(continued)

Practice Text 4-5 *(continued)*

Random Phrases 3 Words Out of Sequence	Random Phrases 3 Words In Sequence	Random Phrases 4 Words Out of Sequence	Random Phrases 4 Words In Sequence
awareness raise poverty	raise poverty awareness	long the path dusty	the long dusty path
necessary reading is	reading is necessary	help awareness poverty raise	help raise poverty awareness
the from audience	from the audience	see replay game in	see game in replay
great a story	a great story	being progress is made	progress is being made
are flights scheduled	flights are scheduled	are decisions quickly made	decisions are made quickly
changes planning for	planning for changes	basic business has plan	has basic business plan
provided training office	office training provided	awareness help raise public	help raise public awareness
the from top	from the top	regular on a basis	on a regular basis
regular his pattern	his regular pattern	read an ability to	an ability to read

Practice Text 4-5 *(continued)*

Random Phrases 3 Words Out of Sequence	Random Phrases 3 Words In Sequence	Random Phrases 4 Words Out of Sequence	Random Phrases 4 Words In Sequence
the for project	for the project	looking the at mountain	looking at the mountain
love with her	with her love	friends company the of	friends of the company
morning the in	in the morning	hope one only can	one can only hope
healthy are vegetables	vegetables are healthy	people personal have opinions	people have personal opinions
help money raise	help raise money	trip provisions the for	provisions for the trip
walk taking a	taking a walk	people event the at	people at the event
are values booming	values are booming	hope the best for	hope for the best
world around the	around the world	everyone talent almost has	almost everyone has talent
parade big the	the big parade	the early morning in	in the early morning

Getting the knack for spotting word groups

As your speed reading skills develop, you pick up a knack for locating word groups in sentences and reading them quickly. Exercise 4-6 presents an essay provided by Rogers Historical Museum (Rogers, Arkansas) with the first half divided for you into word groups. Try to read each line (word group) in the first half of Practice Text 4-6 in one glance. When you reach the second half of the essay, you have to identify the word groups on your own; continue trying to read each word group in a single glance.

Practice Text 4-6

In Anglo-American culture
the bride's family
traditionally bears most
of the cost of the wedding
and associated events.
In the 19th and early 20th century
most weddings were low-key and inexpensive,
but the wealthy used a wedding
as yet another opportunity
for conspicuous display
The traditional sequence of events
leading to the wedding
began with a bachelor dinner,
often called a stag party in the 20th century,
and a tea for bridesmaids.
If the wedding was to be
a formal event
then a rehearsal dinner was customary
the night before the wedding itself.
The wedding vows in use by the 1800s
were a combination of
the ancient betrothal and wedding vows
combined into one ceremony.
The giving of a ring to the bride
and the joining of hands
remained part of most wedding ceremonies.
A plain, rather narrow gold ring

Practice Text 4-6 *(continued)*

---

has been the most usual form of wedding ring
in the 1800s and 1900s.
But in the late 19th and early 20th centuries
wide, ornamented bands were common,
while in the 1920s
engraved white gold or platinum bands were fashionable.
World War II finally led American men
to adopt wedding bands
as a symbol of home and family,
and the number of double ring ceremonies increased.
A reception or dinner for guests
traditionally followed the wedding.
In the mid 1800s it was usual to hold the wedding
in the morning followed by
a wedding breakfast and then a lull before an evening dance.

The cutting of the cake has long been the highlight of the reception. In Victorian times the "wedding cake" was the fruitcake cut up and put in fancy boxes to distribute to the guests. The big cake, sometimes tiered, was called the "bride's cake."

Traditionally the bride's cake had a single ring in it, but beginning in the 1920s more and more trinkets were added. Real flowers were the traditional decoration for the bride's cake in the 19th century, while in the 1920s more icing and the bride and groom figures were added.

After the reception the couple would leave for the honeymoon or go directly to their new home. The bride would toss a bouquet to the women, but in Victorian times she threw a special bouquet and kept her own.

The throwing of foodstuffs as a symbol of fertility has been a part of wedding custom for centuries. In the 1800s and into the 1900s rice was usual.

Before World War II the wedding photograph was usually taken before or most often after the wedding in a studio. In the late 1800s and early 1900s the photograph was taken after the wedding but probably in the same clothing.

The traditional pose at the time was the woman standing and the man sitting, with her hand on his shoulder or the chair. By the mid 1900s the couple usually stood side by side.

Taking On Continuous Text

Chapter 8 explores why continuous text like the kind found in newspaper articles is easiest to speed read: because this text is already broken into five-to-ten-word columns that make for natural word groups. You can take in all five to ten words in the column in one eye fixation and therefore can read a newspaper article quickly.

To give you a preview of this skill, Exercise 4-7 contrasts reading text in columns with reading text in blocks (like the text blocks found in this and most other books). The exercise presents the same essay, "What They Don't Teach You in School," in a text block and in columns. You read the essay twice and answer the same comprehension questions after each reading to gauge how much easier the column version is.

Follow these steps to complete the first half of Exercise 4-7:

1. **Timing yourself, read the text-block version of the essay "What They Don't Teach You in School" (Practice Text 4-7a).**

2. **Answer the comprehension questions that follow the text block.**

   You'll answer the same questions again after you finish the second half of the exercise and compare your comprehension.

3. **Record how long you take to read the essay, your word-per-minute (WPM) reading rate, and your effective reading rate (ERR) in Appendix B.**

   Appendix B explains how to calculate your word per minute rate and effective reading rate.

Practice Text 4-7a

What They Don't Teach You in School
by Harvey Mackay, nationally syndicated columnist
Originally published June 17, 2007

As many college graduates are scrambling to find jobs, one of the most important things for graduates to understand is that you're in school all your life. In fact, your real education is just beginning.

I'd like to pass on a few lessons, which weren't necessarily covered in school. If you've been out of school for a few years — or a lot of years — this advice is still for you; consider it a refresher course.

Practice Text 4-7a *(continued)*

Develop relationships and keep networking. If I had to name the single characteristic shared by all the truly successful people I've met over a lifetime, I'd say it is the ability to create and nurture a network of contacts. Start strengthening your relationships now, so they'll be in place when you really need them later. In the classroom it was mostly about your individual performance. Success in real life will require relationships. Who you know determines how effectively you can apply what you know. So stay in touch.

Find advisors and mentors. Advisors will not be assigned to you, as in school. You should actively seek your own mentors. And remember, mentors change over a lifetime. Start connecting with people you respect who can help you get a leg up in each aspect of your life, personal and professional. Make it as easy and convenient as possible for them to talk with you, and always look for ways to contribute to their success, too.

Build your reputation. Nothing is more important than a good reputation in building a successful career or business. If you don't have a positive reputation, it will be difficult to be successful. All it takes is one foolish act to destroy a reputation.

Set goals. Ask any winner what their keys to success are, and you will hear four consistent messages: vision, determination, persistence and setting goals. If you don't set goals to determine where you're going, how will you know when you get there? Goals give you more than a reason to get up in the morning; they are an incentive to keep you going all day. Most important, goals need to be measurable, identifiable, attainable, specific and in writing.

Get along with people. Ask recruiters from various companies to name the number one skill necessary for new hires, and many of them will say it's the ability to get along with people. Co-workers share office space, facilities, break rooms, refrigerators and coffee pots. They arrive together, take breaks together, eat lunch together and meet to solve problems together. All this closeness and familiarity can wear thin at times. Everyone shares responsibility for making the company work, run smoothly and stay profitable

Be happy. We are all responsible for our own happiness. Don't waste time and energy being unhappy. When people aren't happy doing what they do, they don't do it as well. Life will always be filled with challenges and opportunities. Both are best faced with a positive attitude.

(continued)

Practice Text 4-7a *(continued)*

Smile. A smile should be standard equipment for all people. I learned years ago that one of the most powerful things you can do to have influence over others is to smile at them. Everything seems much easier with a smile.

Sense of humor. I'm a firm believer in using humor — not necessarily jokes. A good sense of humor helps to overlook the unbecoming, understand the unconventional, tolerate the unpleasant, overcome the unexpected and outlast the unbearable. There are plenty of times to be serious, but I believe that keeping things light and comfortable encourages better teamwork.

Be yourself. We all have areas that need a little work, but accepting who we are and making the most of our good points will take us much farther than trying to be someone we aren't. Be content with your abilities and comfortable enough in your own skin to trust your gut.

Volunteer. It might be hard to do a lot of volunteer work at first, but people who help other people on a regular basis have a healthier outlook on life. They are more inclined to be go-getters and consistently report being happier. Volunteering is good for everyone.

Now answer the following comprehension questions about the essay — don't forget to come back and answer these questions again after you read the essay in column form. The answer key appears after the second version of the essay (but no peeking until you've completed both parts of the exercise).

Comprehension Questions

1. **What is the single characteristic Harvey MacKay says is shared by all the truly successful people he has met?**

    A. Having a network of contacts

    B. Having goals

    C. Being happy

    D. Having a sense of humor

2. **What is the number one skill necessary for new hires?**

    A. Being happy

    B. Knowing office politics

    C. Getting along with people

    D. Always asking questions

3. **What should you actively seek after you've been out of school for a few years?**

   A. Jobs

   B. Mentors

   C. Funny people

   D. Volunteers

4. **The four consistent messages of winners are vision, determination, persistence and**

   A. Setting goals

   B. Showing up

   C. Working hard

   D. Being happy

5. **Who has a healthier outlook on life?**

   A. Volunteers

   B. Mentors

   C. Recruiters

   D. Advisors

   Answer key: 1: A; **2:** C; **3:** B; **4:** A; **5:** A

"But wait!" you say. "Won't I read the second version faster anyway because I'm already more familiar with it from the first reading?" The answer is most likely yes. However, the benefit you get from reading in columns is still greater than any extra push you get from having seen the text already.

Here's how to complete the second half of Exercise 4-7:

1. **Timing yourself again, read the column version of the same essay (Practice Text 4-7b) and then flip back and answer the comprehension questions again.**

   As you read, try to take in the words in each line with a single glance. Aim your vision at the center of the column and read the words across the column with your peripheral vision.

   As you answer the questions, notice to how much more quickly and confidently you remember the answers.

2. **Write down how long you take to read the column version of the essay and your effective reading rate in Appendix B.**

   Spoiler alert: Reading the essay in column form should take you less time.

Practice Text 4-7b

What They Don't Teach You in School
by Harvey Mackay

As many college graduates are scrambling to find jobs, one of the most important things for graduates to understand is that you're in school all your life. In fact, your real education is just beginning.

I'd like to pass on a few lessons, which weren't necessarily covered in school. If you've been out of school for a few years — or a lot of years — this advice is still for you; consider it a refresher course.

Develop relationships and keep networking. If I had to name the single characteristic shared by all the truly successful people I've met over a lifetime, I'd say it is the ability to create and nurture a network of contacts. Start strengthening your relationships now, so they'll be in place when you really need them later. In the classroom it was mostly about your individual performance. Success in real life will require relationships. Who you know determines how effectively you can apply what you know. So stay in touch.

Find advisors and mentors. Advisors will not be assigned to you, as in school. You should actively seek your own mentors. And remember, mentors change over a lifetime. Start connecting with people you respect who can help you get a leg up in each aspect of your life, personal and professional. Make it as easy and convenient as possible for them to talk with you, and always look for ways to contribute to their success, too.

Build your reputation. Nothing is more important than a good reputation in building a successful career or business. If you don't have a positive reputation, it will be difficult to be successful. All it takes is one foolish act to destroy a reputation.

Set goals. Ask any winner what their keys to success are, and you will hear four consistent messages: vision, determination, persistence and setting goals. If you don't set goals to determine where you're going, how will you know when you get there? Goals give you more than a reason to get up in the morning; they are an incentive to keep you going all day. Most important, goals need to be measurable, identifiable, attainable, specific and in writing.

Get along with people. Ask recruiters from various companies to name the number one skill necessary for new hires, and many of them will say it's the ability to get along with people. Co-workers share office space, facilities, break rooms, refrigerators and coffee pots. They arrive together, take breaks together, eat lunch together and meet to solve problems together. All this closeness and familiarity can wear thin at times. Everyone shares responsibility for making the company work, run smoothly and stay profitable

Be happy. We are all responsible for our own happiness. Don't waste time and energy being unhappy. When people aren't happy doing what they do, they don't do it as well. Life will always be filled with challenges and opportunities. Both are best faced with a positive attitude.

Practice Text 4-7b *(continued)*

Smile. A smile should be standard equipment for all people. I learned years ago that one of the most powerful things you can do to have influence over others is to smile at them. Everything seems much easier with a smile.

Sense of humor. I'm a firm believer in using humor — not necessarily jokes. A good sense of humor helps to overlook the unbecoming, understand the unconventional, tolerate the unpleasant, overcome the unexpected and outlast the unbearable. There are plenty of times to be serious, but I believe that keeping things light and comfortable encourages better teamwork.

Be yourself. We all have areas that need a little work, but accepting who we are and making the most of our good points will take us much farther than trying to be someone we aren't. Be content with your abilities and comfortable enough in your own skin to trust your gut.

Volunteer. It might be hard to do a lot of volunteer work at first, but people who help other people on a regular basis have a healthier outlook on life. They are more inclined to be go-getters and consistently report being happier. Volunteering is good for everyone.

Dollars to doughnuts, it took you about a third less time to read the essay in column form. Why is that? Because reading in columns encourages you to read word group by word group rather than word by word.

If you had trouble with this exercise, you can get more practice by focusing on word groups as you read your newspaper.

Getting Into the Speed-Reading Mindset

Speed reading isn't just a set of techniques for reading faster — it's also a mindset. When you speed read, you read aggressively and with more concentration. Exercise 4-8 focuses you on the speed-reading mindset and its effect on your reading speed. Follow these steps to complete this exercise:

1. **Using a timer, read as much of the essay "Disappointment Is Opportunity in Disguise" (Practice Text 4-8) as you can in 60 seconds.**

2. **When 60 seconds have passed, circle the last word you read.**

3. **Reset the timer, start reading the essay again, and read as far as you can in 50 seconds.**

   Read aggressively with renewed concentration. See whether you can read the same number of words you read in Step 1 in 50 seconds. Being familiar with the text ought to help you break the 50-second mark,

4. **Circle the last word you read when the 50 seconds expired and compare to your 60-second progress.**

   Even if you don't quite reach your earlier stopping point, you may be surprised by just how close you get.

5. **Read the essay a third time for 40 seconds and see whether you can match your progress from Step 3.**

This exercise demonstrates the value of reading aggressively. As you become more confident with your speed reading, you find it easier and easier to adopt the aggressive speed-reading mindset.

Practice Text 4-8

Disappointment Is Opportunity in Disguise
by Harvey Mackay, nationally syndicated columnist
Originally published February 1, 1999

On Super Bowl Sunday, it was a real challenge for me to watch the game at home and not wish I were in Miami losing my voice and cheering for my hometown team, the Minnesota Vikings, to win it all.

Of course, we should have been there. The best offense in football. A record-breaking season for scoring the most points ever. The perfect kicker. The Vegas favorite to win the Super Bowl. And then, ouch! The overtime loss to Atlanta. I've never heard the "Thunderdome" so quiet. Sixty-five thousand silent fans. The disappointment was crushing. We all sat there in shock. We were waiting for something — anything — to make it all better. Not this time. But there's always next year.

Handling disappointment is one of life's little challenges, and often an indication of how we deal with adversity at work as well. Anyone who has been in business can tell war stories about the bumps in the road. But if they've outlasted the competition, ask for their stories about survival. They've figured out how to turn disappointments into opportunities.

Practice Text 4-8 (continued)

Lose one of your best customers? Bummer. But it's not necessarily a defeat. Find out why their orders are going elsewhere. If you messed up, fix what you can and resolve not to make the same mistake again. If the purchasing manager has a new brother-in-law who sells for your competition, well, that's not a disappointment anymore. That's your new challenge. Just don't lower your expectations. If you expect nothing, that's exactly what you'll get. ✓

Didn't get the promotion? Be honest with yourself. Were you right for the job? Was it right for you? Do you have a future with the company? Use your disappointment to do some soul-searching. If there were two qualified people ahead of you, it could be a matter of timing. If you've been passed over before, it's time to quit being disappointed and recognize that you might have to jump to another lily pad. You'll thank your old company later for helping you get out in time.

Take a lesson from James Whitaker, the first American to reach the summit of Mount Everest. Even though he was emotionally ✓ and physically prepared, he encountered more than his share of disappointments: avalanches, dehydration, hypothermia, and the physical and mental fatigue caused by the lack of oxygen at 29,000 feet. Why did Whitaker succeed where so many had given in to their disappointments? "You don't really conquer such a mountain," he said. "You conquer yourself. You overcome the sickness and everything else — your pain, aches, fears — to reach the summit."

Achievers, like Whitaker, focus on the road, rather than the bumps in it, to reach their destination.

Okay, you're on the other side of the desk. Can't find the right person for a job? That's not a disappointment, that's a business emergency. It's time to call in the pros. I use a headhunter and an industrial psychologist for all my key hires. I can't afford to be disappointed.

Is your staff underperforming? Time for another look in the mirror. Perhaps they're as disappointed in you as you are in them. If you can make their job more satisfying . . . challenging . . . rewarding, do it. The results won't disappoint you.

(continued)

Practice Text 4-8 *(continued)*

Next time you're on the golf course, pick up your golf ball and take a close look. The first golf balls manufactured had smooth covers. An avid, but broke, golfer couldn't afford new ones, so he used whatever he found along the course: beat up, nicked golf balls. His playing partners soon noticed that their smooth-covered balls didn't fly as accurately or as far as his. What was going on? But they finally figured out what gave their friend the advantage.

Today, golf balls have as many as 432 dimples. The "rough spots" enhance the ball's distance and accuracy.

Life's like that: rough spots sharpen our performance. And more often than not, the obstacles can be turned into advantages. You just can't let your disappointment get in the way.

Part II

Focusing on the Fundamentals

The 5th Wave   By Rich Tennant

"I can buy the eye holes helping with visual acuity and word clumping, but the cleaver's just to unnerve your sister."

In this part...

This part explores the handful of fundamental skills you need to be a great speed reader. It also offers tons of hands-on practice in mastering those fundamentals — it's your chance to really get going as a speed reader.

Chapter 5 provides your first speed-reading test to find out how fast a reader you are. Chapter 6 shows how to expand your reading vision to take in several words at a time as you read. Chapter 7 looks into the cognitive aspect of speed reading, demonstrating how to read for the author's thoughts and not just her words.

Chapter 5

Establishing Your Reading Rate

How fast do you read? In this chapter, you get a definitive answer. I present two speed-reading tests so that you know your words-per-minute (WPM) reading rate and your effective reading rate (ERR).

You also find out where you stand as a speed reader and how much practice you need to keep improving. You discover how the experts calculate reading speeds and how you can calculate your speed. This chapter also demonstrates how you can dramatically improve your speed just by changing your mindset before you begin reading. Use Appendix B to log your scores and chart your progress.

How the Experts Test Speed-Reading Rates

Experts use two techniques to test how fast people read. One technique measures how many words you read per minute; the other test takes into account how well you comprehend what you read as well as how fast you read. Knowing both rates is helpful. The word-per-minute test gives a raw measure of how fast you read, and the comprehension tests keep you honest by making sure you understand the author's words as well as read quickly. The following sections describe these techniques, and then the rest of this chapter helps you determine your scores.

Throughout this book, I have you calculate and write down your ERR and WPM rate. Fold down the corner of this page. If you find yourself scratching your head and struggling to remember how to calculate the rates, head back here for a refresher. Or go to Appendix B, which also explains how to calculate ERR and WPM scores.

Words per minute (WPM) testing

The *WPM test* isn't very different from a typing test. All it measures is how many words you read per minute. Experts use the following formula to get the results for a WPM reading test:

Words read ÷ reading time in minutes = WPM rate

For example, someone who takes 2 minutes to read 700 words reads at a 350 WPM rate:

700 ÷ 2 = 350

Someone who takes 2.25 minutes (2 minutes, 15 seconds) to read 700 words reads at a 311 WPM rate:

700 ÷ 2.25 = 311

Above-average readers read at a 300 to 700 WPM rate. Spead readers can read more than 700 words per minute.

Effective reading rate (ERR) testing

"I took a speed reading course once," Woody Allen said. "We read *War and Peace* in 20 minutes. It was about Russia." For an ERR test, though, Woody Allen and his classmates would have to answer questions about the Tolstoy novel they read as well as report how fast they read it.

The *effective reading rate* (ERR) measures comprehension as well as speed. ERR testing is a more thorough measure of speed-reading rates than WPM testing (discussed in the previous section) because it tests comprehension, retention, and recall. The test also indicates how strong your vocabulary is and the knowledge reserves that you bring to the table when you start reading.

Experts use the following formula to get the results of an ERR test:

WPM rate × comprehension percentage score (as decimal) = ERR

Someone who reads 700 words at 350 WPM and answers 80 percent of the comprehension questions correctly reads at a 280 ERR rate:

350 × .8 = 280

Effective readers should score at least 80 percent on the comprehension test.

Establishing Your Base Reading Rate

Get ready to jump in and take your first speed-reading test. This test establishes your starting rate so you can see how fast a reader you are and how much you improve in the course of your speed-reading studies.

For this test, read without adopting any of the speed-reading principles you may have already read about in this book. Read as though you don't know anything about speed reading. The idea is to get your base speed-reading rate.

Follow these steps to take your first speed-reading test in Exercise 5-1:

1. **Using a clock, watch, or stopwatch, note what time you begin reading.**

2. **Read "John F. Kennedy's Inaugural Address" (Practice Text 5-1).**

3. **Record how long you take to read the speech and then consult Table 5-1 to get your WPM rate.**

   If your reading time doesn't match one in the chart (or you just want to brush up on your math skills), you can also determine your WPM rate by dividing 1447 (the number of words in the speech) by the amount of time you spent reading it. If you get a number with a decimal (such as 723.5), round up to the next number.

4. **Answer the comprehension questions without revisiting the essay and note how many questions you answer correctly (0, 20, 40, 60, 80, or 100 percent of the questions).**

5. **Use the percentage from Step 4 to find your ERR in Table 5-1.**

   Alternately, you can multiply your WPM rate from Step 3 by 0, .2, .4, .6, .8, or 1 based on the percentage of questions you answered correctly.

6. **Enter your WPM rate and ERR for this reading selection on the worksheet in Appendix B.**

Practice Text 5-1

John F. Kennedy's Inaugural Address

We observe today not a victory of party but a celebration of freedom — symbolizing an end as well as a beginning — signifying renewal as well as change for I have sworn before you and Almighty God the same solemn oath our forbears prescribed nearly a century and three-quarters ago.

The world is very different now, for man holds in his mortal hands the power to abolish all forms of human poverty and all forms of human life. And yet the same revolutionary beliefs for which our forbears fought are still at issue around the globe — the belief that the rights of man come not from the generosity of the state but from the hand of God. We dare not forget today that we are the heirs of that first revolution.

Let the word go forth from this time and place — to friend and foe alike — that the torch has been passed to a new generation of Americans — born in this century, tempered by war, disciplined by a hard and bitter peace, proud of our ancient heritage — and unwilling to witness or permit the slow undoing of those human rights to which this nation has always been committed, and to which we are committed today — at home and around the world.

Let every nation know — whether it wishes us well or ill — that we shall pay any price, bear any burden, meet any hardship, support any friend, oppose any foe, to assure the survival and the success of liberty. This much we pledge — and more.

To those old allies whose cultural and spiritual origins we share: we pledge the loyalty of faithful friends. United — there is little we cannot do in a host of co-operative ventures. Divided — there is little we can do — for we dare not meet a powerful challenge, at odds, and split asunder. To those new states whom we welcome to the ranks of the free: We pledge our word that one form of colonial control shall not have passed away merely to be replaced by a far more iron tyranny. We shall not always expect to find them supporting our view. But we shall always hope to find them strongly supporting their own freedom — and to remember that — in the past — those who foolishly sought power by riding the back of the tiger ended up inside. To those people in the huts and villages of half the globe struggling to break the bonds of mass misery: We pledge our best efforts to help them help themselves, for whatever period is required — not because the Communists may be doing it, not because we seek their votes, but because it is right. If a free society cannot help the many who are poor, it cannot save the few who are rich.

Practice Text 5-1 *(continued)*

To our sister republics south of our border: We offer a special pledge — to convert our good words into good deeds — in a new alliance for progress — to assist free men and free governments in casting off the chains of poverty. But this peaceful revolution of hope cannot become the prey of hostile powers. Let all our neighbors know that we shall join with them to oppose aggression or subversion anywhere in the Americas — and let every other power know that this hemisphere intends to remain the master of its own house.

To that world assembly of sovereign states: The United Nations — our last best hope in an age where the instruments of war have far outpaced the instruments of peace, we renew our pledge of support — to prevent it from becoming merely a forum for invective — to strengthen its shield of the new and the weak — and to enlarge the area in which its writ may run.

Finally, to those nations who would make themselves our adversaries, we offer not a pledge but a request: that both sides begin anew the quest for peace; before the dark powers of destruction unleashed by science engulf all humanity in planned or accidental self-destruction. We dare not tempt them with weakness. For only when our arms are sufficient beyond doubt can we be certain beyond doubt that they will never be employed. But neither can two great and powerful groups of nations take comfort from our present course — both sides overburdened by the cost of modern weapons, both rightly alarmed by the steady spread of the deadly atom, yet both racing to alter that uncertain balance of terror that stays the hand of Mankind's final war.

So let us begin a new — remembering on both sides that civility is not a sign of weakness, and sincerity is always subject to proof. Let us never negotiate out of fear, but let us never fear to negotiate. Let both sides explore what problems unite us instead of belaboring those problems which divide us. Let both sides, for the first time, formulate serious and precise proposals for the inspection and control of arms — and bring the absolute power to destroy other nations under the absolute control of all nations. Let both sides seek to invoke the wonders of science instead of its terrors. Together let us explore the stars, conquer the deserts, eradicate disease, tap the ocean depths, and encourage the arts and commerce. Let both sides unite to heed in all corners of the earth the command of Isaiah — to "undo the heavy burdens — let the oppressed go free."

(continued)

Practice Text 5-1 *(continued)*

And if a beachhead of co-operation may push back the jungle of suspicion — let both sides join in creating not a new balance of power — but a new world of law — where the strong are just — and the weak secure — and the peace preserved . . . .

All this will not be finished in the first one hundred days. Nor will it be finished in the first one thousand days — nor in the life of this administration, nor even perhaps in our lifetime on this planet. But let us begin.

In your hands, my fellow citizens — more than mine — will rest the final success or failure of our course. Since this country was founded, each generation of Americans has been summoned to give testimony to its national loyalty. The graves of young Americans who answered the call to service surround the globe. Now the trumpet summons us again — not as a call to bear arms, though arms we need — not as a call to battle — though embattled we are — but a call to bear the burden of a long twilight struggle — year in and year out, rejoicing in hope, patient in tribulation — a struggle against the common enemies of man: tyranny — poverty — disease — and war itself. Can we forge against these enemies a grand and global alliance — North and South — East and west — that can assure a more fruitful life for all mankind? Will you join in that historic effort?

In the long history of the world, only a few generations have been granted the role of defending freedom in its hour of maximum danger; I do not shrink from this responsibility — I welcome it. I do not believe that any of us would exchange places with any other people or any other generation. The energy, the faith, the devotion which we bring to this endeavor will light our country and all who serve it — and the glow from that fire can truly light the world.

And so, my fellow Americans — ask not what your country can do for you — ask what you can do for your country. My fellow citizens of the world — ask not what America will do for you, but what together we can do for the Freedom of Man.

Finally, whether you are citizens of America or citizens of the world, ask of us here the same high standards of strength and sacrifice which we ask of you. With a good conscience our only sure reward, with history the final judge of our deeds; let us go forth to lead the land we love, asking His blessing and His help, but knowing that here on earth God's work must truly be our own.

Comprehension Questions

1. **What does man have in his mortal hands the power to abolish all forms of?**

    A. Human poverty and human life

    B. Human dignity and human life

    C. Human life and human intelligence

    D. Human poverty and human dignity

2. **What does Kennedy pledge to not replace colonial control with?**

    A. Absolute tyranny

    B. Unrepentant tyranny

    C. Iron tyranny

    D. Iron democracy

3. **What animal does Kennedy refer to when mentioning those who foolishly sought power?**

    A. Lion

    B. Elephant

    C. Panther

    D. Tiger

4. **What is not a sign of weakness?**

    A. Sincerity

    B. Civility

    C. Democracy

    D. Capitalism

5. **What is the only sure reward Kennedy speaks of?**

    A. A good conscience

    B. An absolute guarantee

    C. A certain victory

    D. A sure victory

Answers: 1: A; **2:** C; **3:** D; **4:** B; **5:** A

Table 5-1		Effective Reading Rates				
Time (Minutes)	WPM	Effective Reading Rate				
		20%	40%	60%	80%	100%
1	1447	289	579	868	1158	1447
1.25	1158	232	463	695	926	1158
1.5	965	193	386	579	772	965
1.75	827	165	331	496	661	827
2	724	145	289	434	579	724
2.25	643	129	257	386	514	643
2.5	579	116	232	347	463	579
2.75	526	105	210	316	421	526
3	482	96	193	289	386	482
3.25	445	89	178	267	356	445
3.5	413	83	165	248	331	413
3.75	386	77	154	232	309	386
4	362	72	145	217	289	362
4.25	340	68	136	204	272	340
4.5	322	64	129	193	257	322
4.75	305	61	122	183	244	305
5	289	58	116	174	232	289
5.25	276	55	110	165	220	276
5.5	263	53	105	158	210	263
5.75	252	50	101	151	201	252
6	241	48	96	145	193	241
6.25	232	46	93	139	185	232
6.5	223	45	89	134	178	223
6.75	214	43	86	129	171	214
7	207	41	83	124	165	207

Seeing Where You Stand as a Speed Reader

After you know your WPM rate and your ERR, you may be curious to know how you compare to others in the speed-reading department. (And who wouldn't be?)

Roughly speaking, readers fall into these categories where speed is concerned:

- ✔ **1 to 200 WPM:** You're a talker. You read one word at a time at about the same speed as you talk and you may move your lips when you read. Most talkers are held back because they engage in *vocalization* while they read — they speak the words silently to themselves as they read them. Unless you're an especially fast talker, reading at the speed you talk slows you down.

- ✔ **200 to 300 WPM:** You're an average reader, one who probably doesn't enjoy reading as a hobby. You engage in some vocalization as you read, but you can read several words at once. Most people read at this speed.

- ✔ **300 to 700 WPM:** You're an above average reader who can read groups of words in a single glance, recognizing and reading phrases in sentences quickly. You vocalize a little when you read. You very likely have a large vocabulary.

- ✔ **700+ WPM:** You're a speed reader. You're adept at reading 10 to 16 words at a glance, both horizontally and vertically on the page. You read with a great degree of confidence and agility.

So if your ERR (established in the previous section) is 700 or above, take the rest of the day off and give yourself a raise while you're at it. You don't need speed-reading lessons — you're already a fast reader. If your ERR isn't as high as you want, keep reading.

Chapter 6

Taking in More than One Word at a Time: Reading in Clumps

In This Chapter

▶ Discovering what clumps are (and that you can already read them)

▶ Seeing words as shapes and images when you read

▶ Understanding macular and peripheral vision

▶ Changing your mindset when you read in clumps

▶ Developing your clump-reading ability

This chapter introduces the concept of reading in clumps, a necessary skill for speed readers. Loosely speaking, a clump is any collection of words that appear together on the page.

In this chapter, you find out what clump reading entails, how the eyes and mind work when you read in clumps, and how to make the shift from one-word-at-a-time reading to clump reading. I also give you many exercises that let you try your hand (okay, eyes) at clump reading.

What Is a Clump, Anyway?

Reading in clumps means to take in more than one word at a time in the course of your reading. A *clump* is a collection of 4 to 16 next-to-each-other words that you read in a single glance (or *eye fixation,* discussed in Chapter 3). When you read in clumps, you naturally increase your speed because you can't slow down to *vocalize* (speak or hear the words as you read them). After all, you can't speak 4 to 16 words at a time without slurring the words or turning them into corned beef hash.

Being able to read in clumps is an essential skill for speed readers. Throughout this book, you discover tricks for dividing the words you read into clumps. For example, in Chapter 7, you see how to recognize a prepositional phrase in the text as part of a clump and read it in one gulp. In this chapter, however, you just need to know that any group of 4 to 16 words can be read quickly as a clump. All you need is practice.

If the notion of reading in clumps seems odd or impossible, consider this point: If you read a newspaper or religious text, you already know how to read in clumps.

Newspapers are laid out in narrow columns, and each column is essentially a clump. Text in holy books such as the Bible and Koran always appears in columns as well. When you read text in columns, you're prone to read in clumps, and that increases your reading speed.

To see the advantages of reading in clumps, read the following news story "Dramatic Cat Rescue on Green Street" by Peter Weverka. It gives you hands-on experience in reading text in different-sized columns.

1. **First, read the story as a single block of text.**

   Later, you compare how fast you read text in blocks to how fast you read text in columns.

Dramatic Cat Rescue on Green Street — block text

Pinkertown (August 14) — Residents of Green Street witnessed the noon rescue of a cat by firefighters yesterday. The cat, a tabby, was heard mewling in the branches of an elm tree for more than an hour before firefighters arrived on the scene and brought the cat down from a high branch with the use of a hook and ladder truck.

Two dozen witnesses burst into applause as the cat was rescued. The cat, Samantha, ran to the arms of its owner, Roberta Haynes Johannsen, after it was carried down from the tree.

"Samantha is always climbing up that tree, but this is the first time she wasn't able to get down," said Johannsen. "I would like to thank my neighbors for alerting the fire department. I was in back tending to my garden and didn't hear Samantha's cries."

This was the fourth time this year that the fire department was called upon to rescue a cat from a tree, according to Sergeant Dale Martinez, who supervised the rescue. "We don't train our firefighters to rescue cats," he said, "but we're pretty good at it. Cats seem to like firefighters."

Cats climb trees to avoid other cats and dogs, and to chase animals such as squirrels. However, the animals are more adept at climbing up than climbing down trees. Sometimes they get trapped on a high branch and are unable to come down unassisted.

"I hope Samantha has learned her lesson," said Johannsen. "I wouldn't want her to get caught in that tree again."

2. **Now, read the text divided into columns.**

Notice how the columns encourage you to jump ahead in your reading. You can take in more words at a time. You can read in clumps.

**Dramatic Cat Rescue
on Green Street — column text**

Pinkertown (August 14) — Residents of Green Street witnessed the noon rescue of a cat by firefighters yesterday. The cat, a tabby, was heard mewling in the branches of an elm tree for more than an hour before firefighters arrived on the scene and brought the cat down from a high branch with the use of a hook and laddertruck. Two dozen witnesses burst into applause as the cat was rescued. The cat, Samantha, ran to the arms of its owner, Roberta Haynes Johannsen, after it was carried down from the tree. "Samantha is always

(continued)

climbing up that tree, but this is the first time she wasn't able to get down," said Johannsen. "I would like to thank my neighbors for alerting the fire department. I was in back tending to my garden and didn't hear Samantha's cries." This was the fourth time this year that the fire department was called upon to rescue a cat from a tree, according to Sergeant Dale Martinez, who supervised the rescue. "We don't train our firefighters to rescue cats," he said, "but we're pretty good at it. Cats seem to like firefighters." Cats climb trees to avoid other cats and dogs, and to chase animals such as squirrels. However, the animals are more adept at climbing up than climbing down trees. Sometimes they get trapped on a high branch and are unable to come down unassisted.

"I hope Samantha has learned her lesson," said Johannsen. "I wouldn't want her to get caught in that tree again."

3. **Finally, read the third version of the text, which has a line drawn on the page to simulate columns.**

As you read, focus on the text on either side of the line as though you were reading it in columns. In other words, read in clumps. When you speed read, you can try mentally drawing column lines like the one shown here so that you can read in clumps.

Dramatic Cat Rescue on Green Street — divided text

Pinkertown (August 14) — Residents of Green Street witnessed the noon rescue of a cat by firefighters yesterday. The cat, a tabby, was heard mewling in the branches of an elm tree for more than an hour before firefighters arrived on the scene and brought the cat down from a high branch with the use of a hook and ladder truck.

Two dozen witnesses burst into applause as the cat was rescued. The cat, Samantha, ran to the arms of its owner, Roberta Haynes Johannsen, after it was carried down from the tree.

"Samantha is always climbing up that tree, but this is the first time she wasn't able to get down," said Johannsen. "I would like to thank my neighbors for alerting the fire department. I was in back tending to my garden and didn't hear Samantha's cries."

This was the fourth time this year that the fire department was called upon to rescue a cat from a tree, according to Sergeant Dale Martinez, who supervised the rescue. "We don't train our firefighters to rescue cats," he said, "but we're pretty good at it. Cats seem to like firefighters."

Cats climb trees to avoid other cats and dogs, and to chase animals such as squirrels. However, the animals are more adept at climbing up than climbing down trees. Sometimes they get trapped on a high branch and are unable to come down unassisted.

"I hope Samantha has learned her lesson," said Johannsen. "I wouldn't want her to get caught in that tree again."

Reading text in columns really is easier. I sometimes wonder why publishers don't present text in columns in biographies and novels, for example. Column text encourages you to read faster.

Comprehending Clump-Reading Mechanics

You can read words in clumps because you read with your peripheral vision as well as your macular vision. By training yourself to use both types of vision when you read, you can become a speed reader. These pages explain how macular and peripheral vision work so that you get a better idea of how to become a speed reader.

Macular and peripheral vision

Even when you're not reading, you see with two types of vision:

- ✔ **Macular vision** is your primary focus. When you look directly at something, you see with your macular vision. It comes to you courtesy of the *macula* (an area of particularly sharp vision) of the retina in your eyes.

- ✔ **Peripheral vision** is what you see less distinctly in the area outside your macular vision. Because receptor cells on the retina of your eye are concentrated at the center and are less concentrated toward the edges, colors and shapes are harder to distinguish in peripheral vision (although you can quickly pick up on motion). But you can see to the left, to the right, above, and below the area bordered by your macular vision.

To understand the difference between your macular and peripheral vision, try this short activity:

1. **Hold a pencil about 12 inches in front of your nose and stare at the pencil so it's fully in focus.**

   What you see is the result of your macular vision.

2. **Without gazing away from the pencil, notice the objects outside your macular vision.**

   These objects appear in your peripheral vision. Although they aren't as sharply in focus as the pencil, you can see them.

3. **Pick an object outside your macular vision and try to see it but still see the pencil.**

   If you can do this without crossing your eyes, you can read clumps with your peripheral vision.

Reading with your peripheral vision too

When you read in clumps, you read words in your peripheral as well as your macular vision. Horizontally, you read words to the left and right of your macular vision; vertically, you read words above and below your macular vision.

Training yourself to use your peripheral vision when reading isn't a matter of improving your eyesight but rather of reading with more concentration and focus. As well as taking in what you see in your macular vision, you extend your eye span to take in what is in your peripheral vision.

Using your peripheral vision allows you to read with fewer eye fixations because your vision span is wider and you can see, read, and process more words at a time. Instead of reading word-for-word, you can jump ahead by several words and read in clumps. For example, consider this sentence:

A thing of beauty is a joy forever.

If you read the sentence one word at a time, you read it like this:

A — thing — of — beauty — is — a — joy — forever.

But if you read it as a clump, making use of your peripheral vision as you read, you can focus on the word (or words) at the center of the sentence and rely on your peripheral vision to take in the words on either side. In this instance, your macular vision focuses on the word *beauty,* and your peripheral vision perceives the other words. Try focusing on the italicized word and taking in the other words with your peripheral vision:

A thing of *beauty* is a joy forever.

For Exercise 6-1, use a pacer to move down the columns in Practice Text 6-1, reading the numbers. Focus on the underlined digit(s) in the center of each number, and rely on your peripheral vision to read the number in its entirety. Doing so demonstrates how you can stretch your vision span and use your peripheral vision to read faster.

Practice Text 6-1

2<u>1</u>9	48<u>7</u>57	17<u>77</u>012	472<u>155</u>592
4<u>0</u>4	40<u>2</u>58	17<u>35</u>677	404<u>484</u>541
1<u>1</u>7	10<u>8</u>89	31<u>04</u>730	134<u>391</u>247
4<u>3</u>4	41<u>5</u>70	29<u>96</u>099	475<u>050</u>907
1<u>8</u>1	34<u>0</u>80	22<u>31</u>983	338<u>292</u>110
1<u>6</u>5	45<u>1</u>44	27<u>92</u>935	213<u>530</u>153
3<u>8</u>5	17<u>4</u>31	14<u>32</u>349	400<u>821</u>900
2<u>1</u>9	42<u>3</u>38	18<u>86</u>022	483<u>013</u>940
4<u>0</u>8	36<u>9</u>25	15<u>11</u>155	266<u>725</u>952

(continued)

Practice Text 6-1 *(continued)*			
186	32096	3776587	302469400
278	49718	4364217	271893733
222	20335	4019393	409082071
466	33005	2897962	108704426
129	10233	1145000	205252586
309	11632	3274875	240595606
435	27011	1397779	452501301
102	11854	3938991	447278735
264	10488	1166005	256367626
306	21816	3440952	169777489
335	13172	4377133	153158790
907	29198	4190549	135771536
113	20994	2551421	263506871
235	29542	4071720	148810085
310	49294	2740323	475604744
177	10916	2135077	129793145
494	14658	1175610	193522247
211	31026	4052701	375911510
243	14132	2480556	435964373
128	27724	1009626	313588345
210	17943	1065742	323235821
207	32662	1224748	450624949
418	28797	2362104	243367936
250	23194	3927105	456518103
452	35647	1363576	410443493

Practice Text 6-1 *(continued)*			
1<u>2</u>5	20<u>0</u>98	46<u>26</u>397	383<u>484</u>029
8<u>0</u>5	25<u>8</u>86	12<u>60</u>865	231<u>855</u>246
4<u>7</u>8	36<u>2</u>96	48<u>26</u>513	421<u>024</u>561
2<u>2</u>1	20<u>3</u>92	46<u>70</u>800	453<u>394</u>637
1<u>1</u>7	20<u>5</u>32	18<u>17</u>066	132<u>954</u>739
4<u>3</u>8	36<u>9</u>12	18<u>48</u>698	404<u>758</u>835

Recognizing images as words

Reading words in clumps is possible because when you read most words, you don't see the letters in the words or the words per se. What you see on the page are images that you recognize from your past reading experience — that is, the words are in your vocabulary.

The only time you actually see a word and examine all its letters is the first few times you encounter it. You have to examine the letters closely and commit the word to memory. After it becomes a part of your vocabulary, you can recognize its image. You can identify and process it quickly as part of a clump in the course of your reading.

Another example of recognizing a word as an image or shape is what happens when your name appears in print and your eye immediately jumps to it. Even if your name is buried in the middle of a paragraph, you see it instantly. You can see it right away because the image formed by the letters in your name, not your name itself, is instantly recognizable to you.

A capital I-dea

In English, the first-person singular pronoun *I* is always capitalized for a reason (and not just because English speakers have big egos). Capitalizing the word *I* became a spelling convention to make reading easier. The shape of the capital letter *I* is much easier to recognize than the shape of the lowercase *i.*

A word by any other shape . . .

In 1976, Graham Rawlinson, a researcher at Nottingham University, conducted an experiment to uncover what information readers get from letters and words when reading. He had volunteers read sentences in which the letters in the words were jumbled except for the first and last letters. For example, the word *important* would be spelled *inrmoatpt,* with the initial letter *i* and final letter *t* in the right places but all other letters mixed up or (to use the scientific term) randomized.

What Rawlinson discovered was surprising: People could read and comprehend the jumbled words almost as easily as unjumbled words. The experiment showed, Rawlinson wrote in *New Scientist* magazine, "that randomising letters in the middle of words had little or no effect on the ability of skilled readers to understand the text."

Try this experiment yourself. Read the following paragraphs at normal speed. See whether you can understand the words as easily as you can understand words that aren't jumbled.

> Rseaerch icntidaes taht the oerdr of the ltteers in a wrod dnsoe't mettar. Waht relaly mtteras is the frist and lsat leettr in the wrod. If tehy are in the rhgit palce, you can raed the wdors.

> Wehn you raed, you dno't raed evrey leettr in ecah wrod. You look at the wrod as a wlohe.

If you're a typical reader, you were you able to read the paragraphs without any trouble. This experiment suggests that

✓ You read words as a whole when you read, not letter by letter.

✓ The first and last letter of a word may be the most important letters for recognizing a word because these letters define the word's shape more than the others, and word shapes matter in reading.

✓ Context plays a role in reading. The words on either side of a word provide meaning to the word, and you can often tell what a word means by reading the words beside it.

✓ If a word is familiar to you, you're capable of recognizing it even if it's misspelled.

The following example demonstrates how you see images, or shapes, when you read, not letters. In the example, you see two identical paragraphs. In the first paragraph, a line is drawn through the top half of the letters; in the second, a line is drawn through the bottom half of the letters.

~~Pinkerton is located between Redville and Whiteborough, in Palette County. The village had a population of 5,873 as of the 2000 census. The major industry of the town is tourism. Of special interest are the Waldorf Caves, located south of the town, and the Pembroke Museum, famous for its Quaker quilts. The annual Moon Festival is held in the second week of June.~~

~~Pinkerton is located between Redville and Whiteborough, in Palette County. The village had a population of 5,873 as of the 2000 census. The major industry of the town is tourism. Of special interest are the Waldorf Caves, located south of the town, and the Pembroke Museum, famous for its Quaker quilts. The annual Moon Festival is held in the second week of June.~~

The first paragraph is difficult to read because the line obscures the shapes made by the letters, and you have to work to decipher the message. The second paragraph, however, is easy to read because you can still see the word shapes and therefore read as you do normally, by observing the shapes and images made by the words. This example shows you that to some degree, reading words is just recognizing shapes.

Making the Shift to Clump Reading

Reading in clumps requires you to make a fundamental shift in the way you read. Instead of merely reading words, you perceive them on the page. You also make peripheral vision a part of your reading and rely on context to give meaning to words you don't know. Earlier in the chapter, I discuss perceiving words as images (in "Recognizing Images as Words") and reading with peripheral vision (in "Comprehending Clump-Reading Mechanics") In the following sections, I show you how those concepts (plus using context clues) set the stage for your speed-reading success.

Changing your relationship to words on the page

In speech, one word always follows another, and the same is true when you read one word at a time. When reading in clumps, however, your eyes are like a camera that can take rapid-fire photographs — your eyes take a snapshot of several words, and your mind processes and understands what the words convey. Reading in clumps is a way of perceiving the words on the page rather than merely reading them. Instead of reading word by word, you read idea by idea. You read aggressively, scouring the page for ideas rather than words.

Widening your reading vision

Reading in clumps requires you to stretch your reading vision. Don't be afraid to aggressively take in several words at a time; instead of beginning a line on the left margin, move the center of your vision — your macular vision — a third of the way into the line and begin reading there. Rely on your peripheral vision to take in the words to the left and right of the word you're focusing on. The same idea applies to the end of a line — use your peripheral vision to take in the last few words instead of reading all the way to the end of the line.

When you read in clumps, you discover how to read a line of text with fewer eye fixations. And to do that, you have to stretch out your reading vision. You have to read with eyes that are wide and ready.

Reading in context

After you train yourself to read in clumps, you discover a remarkable bonus benefit: Your comprehension, retention, and recall improve. Because you take in more words at a time, you don't have to decode each word as you read it. When you read several words at once, each word provides meaning (context) to the words around it, and for that reason, you're less likely to stumble over the meaning of an individual word.

To see the benefits of reading in context, consider this sentence. If you read it one word at a time, you stumble over the word *pedagogy* (assuming you don't already know that word):

> His pedagogy in teaching reading was duly noted by the leading thinkers in the art and science of teaching.

However, if you can read in clumps, you can take in this sentence in two or three glances, and when you get to the end, you see that pedagogy is the art and science of teaching.

This ability to read words in context is one of the primary speed-reading skills — and one of the primary reasons why speed readers can read that much faster with improved comprehension, retention, and recall.

Getting More Practice Reading in Clumps

The remainder of this chapter provides exercises to help you get in the habit of reading in clumps and develop your horizontal and vertical peripheral vision. As you do these exercises, don't be afraid to throw off your blinders and read entire groups of words. Reading in clumps requires a certain amount of daring. Go to it! Be bold if you want to acquire the ability to read it clumps.

Reading clump phrases

At its most basic, a clump is a collection of several words that are next to each other horizontally on the page. Exercise 6-2 gives you practice in reading this basic type of clump to help accustom you to reading in clumps and to expand your reading vision. In Practice Text 6-2, you see clumps ranging from four to eight words, with the centermost words in each clump underlined. Using a pacer, read down the columns. As you come to a new clump, focus first on the underlined words, and try to read the other words with your peripheral vision.

Practice Text 6-2

4-word Clumps	6-word Clumps	8-word Clumps
things always get better	brand new products require extensive planning	his popularity among town voters is very high
watching our children first	ugly movies are released on video	see the game action again in the replay
men in the novel	poor people have their own opinions	vital upbeat people have their own great ideas
more boys are singing	kind thoughts make for good results	all jazz bands will play in weekday concerts
history in the making	background reports on the new situation	most popular movies are available later on video
those items sound interesting	red paint brightens up a home	beautiful views from the top of the boat
you're ready for anything	changing the street at the corner	it is often very dry in the desert
clear ability always counts	in summer we'll celebrate the occasion	only twelve miles to the nearest large city
unforgettable in every way	snow falls everywhere around the world	marketing a product successfully requires a strong strategy
doors sometimes open outward	cruel thoughts make for bad times	yearly reports show that progress is being made
friendly neighbors are welcome	parks are getting better than ever	nearly everyone in town supports the baseball team
kings on the stage	necessity is the mother of invention	no real questions from the audience were answered
stranger than any dream	many words can be learned efficiently	many former legislators later become lobbyists in Washington
women and children first	brilliant flowers in the ladies room	there is a good story to be told

Practice Text 6-2 (continued)

4-word Clumps	6-word Clumps	8-word Clumps
gone are incredible times	the house is in the field	unique advertizing always will help raise poverty awareness
guide dogs come home	every preparation for a weekend trip	representatives of the company were at the event
John's very special event	friendly citizens in towns and villages	late arrivals are always welcome at the meetings
sun in the sky	from the Earth to the moon	charging to the top of the high mountain
always explore your opportunities	eating dinner in an exceptional restaurant	tomorrow an appointment with the company is scheduled
early in the morning	light furniture brightens up every room	x-rays were viewed by doctors at the event
games on the shore	good publicity can be very helpful	eating an early dinner in an elaborate restaurant
huge birds are flying	nothing shines like success in life	property values are slowly rising in the town
deep in the night	everyone has an ability to succeed	making plans for important changes in the company
idea sounds very interesting	movies are not better than before	birds like to sing in the early morning
love around the corner	sixty miles to the nearby town	looking at the star in the north sky
rain is falling hard	jolly movies are released for children	paintings are on permanent exhibition at the museum
no very dark nights	vintage items do lead to memories	quaint ideas cause unique ways to change styles
the night is cold	open the window for fresher ait	go to the next village down the road

Reading sentence clumps

Like Exercise 6-2, Exercise 6-3 expands your reading vision and trains you to read clumps. But brace yourself: Exercise 6-3 is a little bit more challenging. Instead of phrases, you read Chinese fortune cookie fortunes courtesy of www.fortunecookiemessage.com. These clumps consist of whole sentences, not phrases, and in this regard they're more like the clumps you encounter in real-life reading situations.

Move your pacer down the page and focus first on the underlined portion of each fortune in Practice Text 6-3. Try to read the words on either side of the underlined section with your peripheral vision. I hope you have good fortune doing this exercise!

Practice Text 6-3

Never quit!

Take it easy.

Accept yourself.

You <u>love</u> peace.

You <u>like Chinese</u> food.

Face <u>facts with</u> dignity.

Life <u>is a</u> verb.

It's tough <u>to</u> be fascinating.

Listen to <u>yourself</u> more often.

He who <u>seeks</u> will find.

Your success <u>will</u> astonish everyone.

Smile. Tomorrow <u>is</u> another day.

Your passions <u>sweep</u> you away.

Keep your <u>plans</u> secret for now.

Think of <u>mother's</u> exhortations more.

Good beginning <u>is</u> half done.

Plan for <u>many</u> pleasures ahead.

The simplest <u>answer is</u> to act.

Don't just <u>spend time,</u> invest it.

Don't find <u>fault; find</u> a remedy.

Live each <u>day well</u> and wisely.

Everyone <u>agrees you</u> are the best.

Everything <u>will now</u> come your way.

Some pursue <u>happiness; you</u> create it.

You will <u>have a</u> bright future.

Compassion is <u>a way</u> of being.

Consume less. <u>Share more.</u> Enjoy life.

Spring has <u>sprung. Life</u> is blooming.

Humor is <u>an affirmation</u> of dignity.

You will <u>travel to</u> many places.

Great thoughts <u>come from</u> the heart.

Someone is <u>speaking well</u> of you.

You will <u>witness a</u> special ceremony.

You will be <u>successful</u> in your work.

A pleasant surprise <u>is</u> waiting for you.

Your hard work <u>will</u> pay off today.

Widening your vision: Reading horizontal and vertical clumps

Exercise 6-4 takes clump reading to a deeper level. To be a good speed reader, you must be able to read clumps vertically as well as horizontally, so in this exercise, you (surprise!) read in clumps horizontally *and* vertically to give your reading vision a real stretch.

Read down the columns in Practice Text 6-4 with a pacer, focusing your macular vision on the underlined words in each clump and your peripheral vision on the remaining words. (See "Macular and peripheral vision" earlier in this chapter for more on the two components of vision.) Try to take in the entire clump in one glance, whether it's one line long or four. Focus hard on your vision as you complete this exercise. Thanks to Rogers Historical Museum (Rogers, Arkansas) for providing the text.

Practice Text 6-4

1 Word per Eye Fixation (1 Word on 1 Line)	4 Words per Eye Fixation (2 Words on 2 Lines)	6 Words per Eye Fixation (3 Words on 2 Lines)
In	In <u>the</u> 19th century	In the <u>19th</u> <u>century</u> middle and
the		
19th	middle <u>and</u> <u>upper</u> class	upper class <u>girls</u> <u>were</u> educated primarily
century	girls <u>were</u> <u>educated</u> primarily	to be <u>wives</u> <u>and</u> mothers. Romantic
middle		
and	to <u>be</u> <u>wives</u> and	love now <u>was</u> <u>seen</u> as a
upper	mothers. <u>Romantic</u> <u>love</u> now	precondition for <u>marriage</u> <u>and</u> the foundation
class		
girls	was <u>seen</u> <u>as</u> a	upon which <u>its</u> <u>happiness</u> rested. Courtship
were	precondition <u>for</u> <u>marriage</u> and	was strictly <u>governed.</u> <u>Couples</u> "courted" rather
educated		
primarily	the <u>foundation</u> <u>upon</u> which	than "dated," <u>meeting</u> <u>in the</u> girl's home
to	its <u>happiness</u> <u>rested.</u> Courtship	with her <u>parents</u> <u>nearby</u> or going
be		
wives	was <u>strictly</u> <u>governed.</u> Couples	out in <u>groups</u> <u>with</u> a young
and	"courted" <u>rather</u> <u>than</u> "dated,"	<u>married</u> couple along. <u>A</u> serious courtship
mothers.		
Romantic	meeting <u>in</u> <u>the</u> girl's	was expected <u>to</u> <u>end</u> in betrothal,
love	home <u>with</u> <u>her</u> parents	and the <u>man</u> <u>was</u> expected to
now		
was	nearby <u>or</u> <u>going</u> out . . .	propose, traditionally <u>on</u> <u>bended</u> knee. A . . .
seen . . .		

Practice Text 6-4 *(continued)*

9 Words per Eye Fixation (3 Words on 3 Lines)	12 Words per Eye Fixation (3 Words on 4 Lines)	16 Words per Eye Fixation (4 Words on 4 Lines)
In the 19th century middle and upper class girls	In the 19th century middle and upper class girls were educated	In the 19th century middle and upper class girls were educated primarily to be wives and
were educated primarily to be wives and mothers. Romantic	primarily to be wives and mothers. Romantic love now was seen as	mothers. Romantic love now was seen as a precondition for marriage and the foundation upon which
love now was seen as a precondition for marriage	a precondition for marriage and the foundation upon which its happiness rested.	its happiness rested. Courtship was strictly governed. Couples "courted" rather than "dated," meeting in the girl's
and the foundation upon which its happiness rested. Courtship	Courtship was strictly governed. Couples "courted" rather than "dated," meeting in the	home with her parents nearby or going out in groups with a young married couple along.
was strictly governed. Couples "courted" rather than "dated," meeting	girl's home with her parents nearby or going out in groups with	A serious courtship was expected to end in betrothal, and the man was expected to propose,
in the girl's home with her parents nearby or going	a young married couple along. A serious courtship was expected to end	traditionally on bended knee. A young man also was expected to ask his sweetheart's father for
out in groups with a young married couple along.	in betrothal, and the man was expected to propose, traditionally on bended	her hand in marriage. In the late 1800s betrothal became more popularly known as engagement,
A serious courtship was expected to end in betrothal,	knee. A young man also was expected to ask his	and no longer had the moral or legal force that it once had. An engaged couple . . .
and the man was expected to propose, traditionally on	sweetheart's father for . . .	
bended knee. A young man also was expected to . . .		

Chapter 7

Getting the Gist
from Word Groups

In This Chapter

▶ Understanding the difference between clumps and word groups

▶ Seeing different types of word groups as units of meaning

▶ Improving your comprehension by reading word groups

*I*n Chapter 6, you discover how to read in clumps and how reading this way allows you to take in many more words at a time and increase your reading speed. This chapter expands your speed-reading horizons a bit farther and explains how to read word groups. In speed-reading terminology, a *word group* is a set of 4 to 16 words that carry meaning within a reading selection. Reading word group by word group rather than word by word increases your reading comprehension. Word groups are critical because the author's ideas are found in word groups.

This chapter explains in detail what a word group is and how you can quickly recognize word groups on the page. It demonstrates how you can increase your reading speed by leaps and bounds by taking in word groups at the speed with which you read single words. The exercises in this chapter help give you the confidence to read word groups and expand your reading vision so you can read larger and larger word groups.

Going Beyond Clumps to Word Groups

Reading in clumps is the art of taking in 4 to 16 or so words in a single *eye fixation* — in other words, in a single glance. (Chapter 6 demonstrates how clumping words together rather than reading them one at a time increases your reading speed.) A word group is a more sophisticated clump (if you consider something called a "clump" sophisticated.) A word group comprises not just 4 to 16 words, but 4 to 16 words that carry meaning. If you can recognize word groups, you can extract the author's meaning that much more quickly. Because a word group is a unit of meaning, recognizing word groups increases your comprehension as well as improves your speed because you can get the meaning out of the words at the same time as you read them quickly.

To help you understand the difference between clumps and word groups, take a look at these three paragraphs. The paragraphs are identical, but in the second I break the text into clumps, and in the third I break the text into word groups. As you read these paragraphs, try to read the words with a single eye fixation. Notice how reading the clumps in a single eye fixation increases your reading speed, but reading the word groups in a single fixation allows you to get the meaning of the words as well as read them quickly.

Unbroken paragraph:

> Our beach house on the Jersey Shore overlooks a boardwalk that extends for a mile to the north and five miles to the south. All year long when the weather is right, walkers and runners and cyclists pass by. The walkers are by far the most numerous.

Same paragraph broken into clumps:

> Our beach house on the
>
> Jersey Shore overlooks a
>
> boardwalk that extends for a mile
>
> to the north and five
>
> miles to the south.
>
> All year long when the weather is right,
>
> walkers and runners and cyclists pass by.
>
> The walkers are by far the most numerous.

Same paragraph broken into word groups:

> Our beach house
>
> on the Jersey Shore
>
> overlooks a boardwalk
>
> that extends for a mile to the north
>
> and five miles to the south.
>
> All year long

when the weather is right,

walkers and runners and cyclists pass by.

The walkers are by far the most numerous.

The clumps in the second paragraph amount to nothing more than words strung together, but the word groups in the third paragraph have meaning. If you can take in clumps of words with meaning — if you can take in word groups — you can read that much faster and improve your comprehension as well.

Recognizing Word Groups

You can get a head start in recognizing word groups if you remember that word groups are the building blocks that make up every sentence in every piece of writing. The word groups are there; you just have to know how and where to look for them in the course of reading. Never fear — the following sections show you that you already know how to pick out some word groups. They also provide some tricks to help you find other, less obvious groups.

Getting the idea from idioms

One of the easiest ways to understand word groups is to consider the idiom. An *idiom* is a figure of speech that you recognize without having to interpret it. *Better safe than sorry*, *take the bull by the horns*, and *there's no place like home* are examples of English idioms.

Every idiom is a word group because it's a single unit of meaning that doesn't have to appear in context with other words for readers to understand its meaning. All a reader has to do is see the first couple of words of an idiom and the rest of the words usually come tumbling into place. You don't have to read all the words because you already know them, which means even slow readers can read idioms quickly.

To see what I mean, read the following idioms. Try to read each one with a single eye fixation. You can probably do it because you're already familiar with these idioms. Just glance at the words and you know their meanings instantly.

Look a gift horse in the mouth

In for a penny, in for a pound

Born with a silver spoon in his mouth

Between the devil and the deep blue sea

A fool and his money are soon parted

A case of the blind leading the blind

Damned if I do and damned if I don't

Looks as if butter wouldn't melt in his mouth

All work and no play make Jack a dull boy

A bird in the hand is worth two in the bush

Fool me once, shame on you; fool me twice, shame on me

Early to bed, early to rise makes a man healthy, wealthy, and wise

Understanding word groups through idioms

The exercise in this section gives you practice in understanding how to read word groups by reading idioms. It demonstrates that you can see, read, and process a word group with a single eye fixation.

For Exercise 7-1, use a pacer and move it down the list as you read the idioms in Practice Text 7-1 courtesy of www.Idiomsite.com. Focusing on the underlined words in the middle of each idiom, try to read each idiom in a single eye fixation. Read each idiom left to right, and then go down to the next one. Push yourself to do this exercise as quickly as possible. Idioms are the easiest word groups to read. Return to this exercise from time to time to practice reading word groups.

Practice Text 7-1

2 Words	3 Words	4 Words
high five	bend <u>over</u> backwards	it's <u>Greek to</u> me
good Samaritan	pass <u>the</u> buck	down <u>to the</u> wire
loose cannon	when <u>pigs</u> fly	let <u>sleeping dogs</u> lie
French kiss	on <u>the</u> fence	on <u>pins and</u> needles
peeping Tom	under <u>the</u> weather	make <u>no bones</u> about
green room	smell <u>a</u> rat	over <u>my dead</u> body
sitting shotgun	queer <u>the</u> pitch	saved <u>by the</u> bell
Ivy League	twenty-<u>three</u> skidoo	an <u>axe to</u> grind

Practice Text 7-1 *(continued)*		
2 Words	**3 Words**	**4 Words**
mumbo jumbo	crack <u>someone</u> up	he <u>lost his</u> head
joshing me	level <u>playing</u> field	up <u>a blind</u> alley
pipe down	pulling <u>your</u> leg	keep <u>your chin</u> up
nest egg	tie <u>the</u> knot	hell <u>in a</u> handbasket
blue moon	use <u>your</u> loaf	the <u>whole nine</u> yards
feeding frenzy	pull <u>the</u> plug	third <u>time's a</u> charm
dark horse	its <u>anyone's</u> call	flash <u>in the</u> pan
full monty	excuse <u>my</u> French	from <u>rags to</u> riches
pig out	know <u>the</u> ropes	close <u>but no</u> cigar
skid row	in <u>your</u> face	water <u>under the</u> bridge
fool's gold	liquor <u>someone</u> up	curiosity <u>killed the</u> cat
graveyard shift	cup <u>of</u> joe	run <u>out of</u> steam
sixth sense	get <u>over</u> it	sick <u>as a</u> dog
devil's advocate	practice <u>makes</u> perfect	raining <u>cats and</u> dogs
hocus pocus	wild <u>and</u> woolly	drink <u>like a</u> fish
funny farm	rise <u>and</u> shine	out <u>of the</u> blue
ring fencing	dropping <u>like</u> flies	high <u>on the</u> hog
hat trick	break <u>a</u> leg	long <u>in the</u> tooth
no way	tongue <u>and</u> cheek	foam <u>at the</u> mouth
no dice	off <u>the</u> record	apple <u>of my</u> eye
gut feeling	buy <u>a</u> lemon	x <u>marks the</u> spot
chow down	kick <u>the</u> bucket	beating <u>around the</u> bush
dry run	wag <u>the</u> dog	lend <u>me your</u> ear

(continued)

Practice Text 7-1 *(continued)*

2 Words	3 Words	4 Words
spitting image	head <u>over</u> heels	on <u>the same</u> page
zero tolerance	rule <u>of</u> thumb	can't <u>cut the</u> mustard
charley horse	in <u>like</u> Flynn	last <u>but not</u> least
cry wolf	mum's <u>the</u> word	chip <u>on his</u> shoulder
eighty six	against <u>the</u> clock	great <u>minds think</u> alike
field day	hit <u>the</u> sack	beat <u>a dead</u> horse
flea market	cast-<u>iron</u> stomach	a <u>blessing in</u> disguise
baker's dozen	cross <u>your</u> fingers	pedal <u>to the</u> metal
dead ringer	off <u>the</u> hook	pig <u>in a</u> poke

5 Words	6 Words
a slap <u>on</u> the wrist	to make <u>a long</u> story short
come hell <u>or</u> high water	drastic times <u>call for</u> drastic measures
new kid <u>on</u> the block	hit the <u>nail on</u> the head
Elvis has <u>left</u> the building	be careful <u>what you</u> wish for
you are <u>what</u> you eat	from the <u>sublime to</u> the ridiculous
blood is <u>thicker</u> than water	like a <u>fish out</u> of water
actions speak <u>louder</u> than words	no room <u>to swing</u> a cat
off on <u>the</u> wrong foot	in the <u>heat of</u> the moment
all bark <u>and</u> no bite	failure is <u>the mother</u> of success
the drop <u>of</u> a hat	your guess <u>is as</u> good as mine
have an <u>axe</u> to grind	in the <u>twinkling of</u> an eye
the best <u>of</u> both worlds	face only <u>a mother</u> could love
everything but <u>the</u> kitchen sink	the ball <u>is in</u> your court

---

Practice Text 7-1 *(continued)*

5 Words	6 Words
back to <u>the</u> drawing board	go down <u>like a</u> lead balloon
he's high <u>as</u> a kite	bark is <u>worse than</u> their bite
taste of <u>your</u> own medicine	variety is <u>the spice</u> of life
when it <u>rains,</u> it pours	like taking <u>candy from</u> a baby
a chip <u>on</u> your shoulder	idle hands <u>are the</u> devil's tools
Van Gogh's <u>ear</u> for music	wear your <u>heart on</u> your sleeve
a drop <u>in</u> the bucket	a leopard <u>can't change</u> his spots
keep body <u>and</u> soul together	every cloud <u>has a</u> silver lining
till the <u>cows</u> come home	you can't <u>take it</u> with you
it takes <u>two</u> to tango	like a <u>cat on</u> hot bricks
add fuel <u>to</u> the fire	faint heart <u>never won</u> fair lady
all in <u>the</u> same boat	bad workers <u>always blame</u> their tools
barking <u>up</u> the wrong tree	not playing <u>with a</u> full deck
get down <u>to</u> brass tacks	if the <u>cap fits,</u> wear it
an arm <u>and</u> a leg	from the <u>bottom of</u> your heart
keep an <u>eye</u> on him	birds of <u>a feather</u> flock together
drive someone <u>up</u> the wall	lead someone <u>up the</u> garden path
go out <u>on</u> a limb	a day <u>late and</u> dollar short
once in <u>a</u> blue moon	quiet tongue <u>keeps a</u> wise head
now it's <u>time</u> to fly	champagne taste <u>on a</u> beer budget
who would've <u>thought</u> of that	it's just <u>what the</u> doctor ordered
she is <u>pulling</u> your leg	the new <u>kid on</u> the block
they are <u>dropping</u> like flies	you've got <u>rocks in</u> your head

Picking out prepositional phrases

A prepositional phrase is another type of word group that you can identify and grasp quickly in the course of reading. A *prepositional phrase* complements another part of a sentence to give it context. You can train yourself to recognize prepositional phrases in sentences and read this kind of word group quickly.

You can spot a prepositional phrase because it almost always begins with one of these words:

> about, above, across, after, against, along, among, around, at, before, behind, below, beneath, beside, between, beyond, by, despite, down, during, except, for, from, in, inside, into, near, off, of, on, onto, out, outside, over, past, through, throughout, till, to, toward, under, underneath, until, up, upon, with, within, without

A prepositional phrase provides *what*, *where*, *when*, *which one*, or *how* information to the rest of the sentence. Consider the prepositional phrases in these sentences and what they convey:

Information	Prepositional phrase
What	The rule *from the home office* says so.
Where	We found the key *on the table*.
When	*After the term ends*, they will go fishing.
Which one	She is the smartest *of them all*.
How	*By working harder*, they finished first.

In the following sentences, I italicize the prepositional phrases. As you read these sentences, read the prepositional phrases with a single eye fixation. In this way, you get practice in picking out prepositional phrases and reading them quickly.

> The book is *on the table*.
>
> *In the south of France,* the weather is good.
>
> We ordered pizza *at the restaurant*.
>
> There was rejoicing *throughout the land*.
>
> I am very tired *of all this bickering*.
>
> *All across the valley* you could see the rainbow.
>
> The letter *from the marketing department* explains it.
>
> She read the book *during class*.
>
> *In addition,* their proposal is the subject *of a peer review*.
>
> The cat will be punished *for chewing* up a new pair *of shoes*.

To recognize prepositional phrases, remember that a prepositional phrase never appears alone as the subject of a sentence. These phrases aren't the main topic of a sentence — they simply complement the important information.

Taking in larger word groups: Reading phrases

Exercise 7-2 helps you recognize the kind of phrases that you see in everyday reading. Get used to the idea of reading three-, four-, and five-word phrases like the kind you read in this exercise. Doing so greatly increases the number of words you can read per minute.

This exercise trains you to take in word groups rather than read word by word. It expands your peripheral vision so you can read word groups more easily and gets you in the habit of reading word groups. (For more on peripheral vision, head to Chapter 3.)

For this exercise, move a pacer down the page, reading the phrases in Practice Text 7-2 as you go along. Try to take in each phrase with a single eye fixation without vocalizing. To help you do that, focus your eyes on the underlined words (where words are underlined). Repeat this exercise from time to time to maintain your reading in word group skills.

Practice Text 7-2

2 Words	3 Words	4 Words
good fishing	spend <u>or</u> deposit	the important backbone report
time passes	gold <u>and</u> silver	looking around the region
taking charge	the <u>town</u> square	maximum rebate for charges
school days	form <u>great</u> friendships	bird in the hand
game player	hit <u>and</u> run	fishing in the lake
paper cuts	an <u>optimal</u> notice	several chapters to consider
new address	learn <u>new</u> words	account ready to go
used furniture	playing <u>with</u> games	trails in the forest
quality works	street <u>of</u> dreams	members of the council

(continued)

Practice Text 7-2 *(continued)*

2 Words	3 Words	4 Words
recent history	happy <u>squash</u> champ	clouds <u>in the</u> sky
voter choices	one <u>more</u> talk	once <u>upon a</u> time
uncontrolled laughter	visiting <u>good</u> friends	long <u>new word</u> today
three years	sooner <u>or</u> later	staring <u>at the</u> window
his society	various <u>nice</u> situations	visiting <u>family on</u> weekends
rocky coast	tattered <u>mourning</u> shrouds	early <u>in the</u> morning
historic house	the <u>winning</u> numbers	animals <u>in the</u> region
twelve days	early <u>morning</u> sunshine	ship <u>in the</u> distance
new reports	oil <u>and</u> gas	the <u>village green</u> square
our stage	making <u>good</u> friends	unnecessary <u>in every</u> way
large opening	many <u>hard</u> returns	more <u>than you</u> knew
upside down	room <u>to</u> grow	somehow <u>it actually</u> works
sensitive situation	explore <u>your</u> ideas	snow <u>on the</u> mansion
recent arrivals	planning <u>a</u> game	trees <u>in the</u> forest
team player	letter <u>from</u> friends	words <u>tell the</u> story
new idea	walk <u>on</u> water	do <u>yourself a</u> favor
influential friend	quarterly <u>banking</u> report	always <u>ready for</u> action
undeveloped land	seventh <u>yearly</u> results	winter, <u>summer, and</u> spring
quality report	up <u>to</u> speed	colors <u>in the</u> rainbow
good nice	fly <u>in</u> formation	tape <u>player and</u> music
plant variety	very <u>serious</u> music	on <u>shore every</u> night
late arrival	the <u>right</u> decision	someone <u>in the</u> neighborhood
two weeks	late <u>at</u> night	breeding <u>cattle for</u> profits

Practice Text 7-2 *(continued)*

2 Words	3 Words	4 Words
untouched lands	fewer <u>plant</u> species	better <u>sooner than</u> later
secondary school	everything <u>is</u> ready	as <u>time goes</u> by
real easy	play <u>tennis</u> outdoors	several <u>choices to</u> consider
newspaper report	singing <u>a</u> song	acting <u>on the</u> stage
night decisions	hot <u>summer</u> days	good l<u>uck good</u> riddance
picture perfect	people <u>have</u> options	motorist <u>in the</u> distance
weekend escape	less <u>summer</u> pay	water <u>in the</u> well
one fortnight	with <u>or</u> without	middle <u>of the</u> door
under place	very <u>simple</u> music	citizens <u>of the</u> town
official notice	open <u>the</u> windows	ready <u>to go</u> west
tape player	millions <u>of</u> dollars	welcome <u>our children</u> first
seventh year	very <u>close</u> friends	an <u>economical new</u> car
town square	washing <u>the</u> grapes	he's <u>one of</u> them
secret base	ready <u>to</u> golf	walking <u>down the</u> road
various situations	disappearing <u>from</u> view	sheep <u>on the</u> hillside
making friends	the <u>village</u> square	walking <u>up the</u> stairs
service rewards	father <u>and</u> son	cold <u>mornings in</u> winter
occasional statement	nice <u>and</u> thin	a <u>very special</u> evening

5 Words	6 Words
business is <u>better</u> than usual	beautiful flowers <u>in the</u> living room
historic homes <u>in</u> the country	something wicked <u>this way</u> comes now
one day <u>at</u> a time	motels are <u>getting better</u> than ever

(continued)

Practice Text 7-2 *(continued)*

5 Words	6 Words
fresh flowers <u>on</u> the table	popular movies <u>are available</u> on video
the snow <u>is</u> falling lightly	around the <u>world in</u> eighty days
can it <u>be</u> good experiences	watch for <u>animals on</u> the highway
medicines are <u>made</u> of this	eating dinner <u>in an</u> enjoyable restaurant
extra players <u>on</u> the field	there is <u>dirt on</u> the window
basic plan <u>for</u> the country	safely on <u>my own</u> two feet
grass fields <u>in</u> all directions	people have <u>opinions on</u> current events
the game <u>has</u> many periods	very hot <u>evening during</u> the summer
in my <u>own</u> two hands	an author <u>can provide</u> many services
beautiful view <u>from</u> the mountain	three horses <u>running in</u> the field
background music <u>for</u> the player	one team <u>has a</u> convincing lead
fishing in <u>a</u> mountain stream	taking it <u>to a</u> dangerous level
grand times <u>enjoyed</u> by all	books are <u>getting worse</u> than before
every day <u>in</u> every way	ten miles <u>to the</u> nearest town
too grand <u>to</u> be true	be ready <u>to accept</u> every opportunity
keep the <u>home</u> fire burning	what a <u>difference a</u> day makes
history tells <u>a</u> different story	a western <u>cruise would</u> be welcome
movie is <u>better</u> than ever	kids look <u>forward to</u> great times
many trees <u>on</u> the mountainside	space pioneers <u>have the</u> right stuff
the truck <u>show</u> opens soon	reading is <u>the key</u> to everything
the time <u>of</u> your life	forty days <u>until the</u> next holiday
taking it <u>to</u> another level	nothing succeeds <u>like success</u> in life
twelve months <u>make</u> one year	the car <u>is in</u> the driveway
boarding pass <u>for</u> the train	background movie <u>for the</u> garden party

Practice Text 7-2 *(continued)*

5 Words	6 Words
an artist <u>on</u> the stage	open the <u>window for</u> fresher air
hot days <u>are</u> here again	secrets are <u>meant to</u> be kept
a story <u>to</u> be typed	a summer <u>vacation would</u> be nice
funny neighbors <u>in</u> the village	necessity is <u>the mother</u> of invention
large circles <u>in</u> the sky	the best <u>times of</u> your life
anyone can <u>play</u> the game	daylight gets <u>longer during</u> the summer
people have <u>their</u> own opinions	brilliant flash <u>in the</u> north sky
business is <u>driven</u> by profit	the unfamiliar <u>can be</u> an adventure
moving to <u>a</u> distant location	eating is <u>the cornerstone</u> of good health
careful preparation <u>is</u> always wise	the village <u>council has</u> open meetings
anybody can <u>phone</u> the gate	the winds <u>blow across</u> the plains
more clouds <u>in</u> the sky	basic business <u>plan for</u> the church
the trial <u>of</u> your life	stock prices <u>go up</u> and down
study along <u>the</u> southern coast	new ideas <u>can lead</u> to changes
trees go <u>in</u> the front	everyone has <u>an ability</u> to succeed
hard days <u>are</u> back again	sixty miles <u>left in</u> the trip
only eleven <u>miles</u> to go	what a <u>day this</u> has been
last stop <u>out</u> of town	questions were <u>taken from</u> the audience
big cloud <u>in</u> the sky	selling often <u>combines ability</u> and talent
often the <u>wind</u> is blowing	everyone has <u>an ability</u> to survive
family member <u>at</u> the event	paintings of <u>major artists</u> are valuable
still a <u>ways</u> to go	the train <u>is arriving</u> on time
finished house <u>on</u> the market	see the <u>ship in</u> the distance

Finding other key phrases

In speech and writing, a phrase is a group of words that functions as a single unit in a sentence. For speed-reading purposes, a *phrase* is a natural word group that provides the context in a sentence. General phrases are a bit harder to recognize than prepositional phrases because you don't necessarily have words such as *at, by, from, on,* and *toward* to clue you in. But if you can develop the ability to see phrases as you read, you can read that much faster.

Roughly speaking, phrases fall into these four groups:

- ✔ **Adjectival phrase:** A group of words that begins with an adjective and modifies a noun. Example: The day *empty of all hope* has arrived.

- ✔ **Adverbial phrase:** A group of words that functions like an adverb to modify the rest of the sentence. Example: I'll wash the car *when I'm good and ready*.

- ✔ **Noun phrase:** A group of words that that begins with a noun or pronoun and, taken together, forms the subject or object of a sentence. Example: *The day the horses were freed* was a happy day.

- ✔ **Verb phrase:** A group of words that begins with a verb and modifies the subject or object of the sentence. Example: The runner crossed the finish line *to take first place*.

In the following sentences, I underline the phrases. Read the phrases in these sentences with a single eye fixation. With a bit of practice, you can recognize phrases in sentences, treat them as word groups, and devour them on the printed page in a single glance.

He was <u>a distinguished gardener</u>.

Teachers are <u>the source of inspiration</u>.

<u>His life was a story</u> <u>based on faith</u>.

<u>The monthly report</u> was submitted too late.

There was <u>no drought</u> <u>for forty years</u>.

<u>The major cost</u> was <u>in the driveway</u>.

<u>That person has</u> <u>a basic business plan</u>.

He <u>plays tennis indoors</u>.

Identifying the Most Important Word Groups: Thought Units

Generally speaking, a *thought unit* is a word group that expresses a complete thought or idea. Every sentence is composed of thought units because every sentence conveys at least one thought. If you can recognize the word groups that convey thought units, you can read these word groups in a single eye fixation and increase your reading comprehension greatly.

Thought units can be difficult to pick out in sentences because you can't look for commas or other punctuation marks in a sentence for guidance in finding them. Instead, you have to develop the ability to quickly examine how the parts of a sentence fit together and locate the weightiest, or meatiest, part of the sentence. In this sentence, for example, notice where the (italicized) thought units are:

> A quick glance at *the menu told us* that, at this particular restaurant, on this particular evening, *dinner would cost a fortune* no matter what we ate and drank.

In the following sentences, I underline the thought units. Notice in these sentences that the thought unit is the part of the sentence that matters most. You can treat this part as a word group and read it quickly in a single glance.

> This is the way to get to the second floor.
>
> After finishing the paint job, the cleanup work began.
>
> To fix the door, you have to first remove all the paint.
>
> To win the game you must know the rules.
>
> Running a marathon requires endurance and commitment.

Reading Word Groups to Increase Comprehension

Reading word groups has a benefit beyond increasing your reading speed: It also increases your comprehension.

When you read by jumping from word group to word group rather than from word to word, one group of words provides meaning to the next group. You don't have to reread or consult a dictionary if you come across a word or phrase you don't understand because the context and meaning of each sentence is more apparent when you read words in groups.

To understand why reading word groups increases your comprehension, consider the following sentences. In these sentences, you see words that you may not understand if you encounter them alone. However, the word groups that accompany these words give them meaning.

> Unfortunately he was sent to the *asylum* because his mental state deteriorated.

> My friend's father was sent to the *mortuary* today; his funeral is set for tomorrow.

> He loves to study the stars; he spends all his free time at the *planetarium*.

> Prof. Jones' *pedagogy* in teaching reading meets the highest standards of the art and science of teaching.

> *Myriad* is a very misused word; "many" would frequently be a more accurate and better-understood substitute.

> His *dilatory* habits caused every event in which he was part to start late.

You don't have to stop your reading or open a dictionary to understand these words because you can infer their meaning in context from the word groups. One group of words gives meaning to other groups. After you get in the habit of reading word groups, you read with confidence because you know that word groups provide meaning and context.

Exercise 7-3 demonstrates why reading one word at a time slows your reading. Move a pacer down the random nonsense phrases in Practice Text 7-3, trying to read each group of words in one glance. You'll get frustrated very quickly. Don't worry about that; keep reading. Don't look at individual words — try to catch the whole word group.

Practice Text 7-3

2 Words	3 Words	4 Words
horses perfect	assured both general	beneath birth goes tea
among honor	march lord meant	lips seem table next
copyright till	advanced countries main	agree help pulled east
addressed talked	habit carried bishop	islands parents control event
given madam	agreed won less	bay dry one self

Practice Text 7-3 *(continued)*

2 Words	3 Words	4 Words
ain't play	lot Indians respect	knees influence scarcely Jack
honor April	comfort effort kings	companion children money population
bell next	night cities wishes	obtain evil their sentence
lay grant	once forces native	possibly frank glance famous
path write	becoming addition grand	blessed party north patience
arms published	song opinion air	text afterwards dare relations
table colonel	months met lot	make memory nature effect
judgment surface	rest for however	saying image forms soil
seek journey	shoulder intention guide	signs dare remove slow
shadow pictures	volume fish weak	thought height fashion struck
than difference	numbers blind inside	plain cut sacred you're
night college	mind Italy thy	loss minds higher faithful
judge spoke	advance pair next	affected constantly handsome worst
closed harm	could girls highest	drove lose moon strength
female chapter	everybody Charles complete	favor take guard beside
freedom eager	guard all agree	ground age edition corps
knees shows	never friendship blue	news members brought fresh
destroyed among	didn't soldiers however	duties members previous error
conscience sin	copyright returned duke	corps million before months
you pulled	York gave born	two greatest without look
thing ten	when sorry close	troops calling course stream
rising final	period equivalent soldier	raised error often kindness
surrounded Europe	sick sand crowd	story ears degree broad

(continued)

Practice Text 7-3 *(continued)*

2 Words	3 Words	4 Words
sending story	sand Europe fought	shore permission poet stairs
see over	putting captain honest	sad dream otherwise mademoiselle
circle names	breath great failed	chair prevent behind dear
audience cash	evil place they	finger evidence taste forehead
fight attention	age warranties answer	anybody project suggestion look
age hotel	god government singing	golden waited empty then
fought pure	handsome national supply	Italy provided secretary clean
grant forms	must add these	national talking absolutely think
justice himself	game facts up	glass stage generally temple
fortune report	continue first home	conscience delight run medium
beg uncle	chapter judge circumstances	closely half brave hope
sorry laughed	showing best protection	situation Christian majesty yesterday
youth yet	your group reading	works knees suggested from
powerful nut	ought tired or	presence win brilliant wind
tired proposed	where angry firm	troubled say wounded dust
hidden animals	killed ball best	kind within worse shook
ready really	particularly immense near	promised increased remarkable help
fear pope	empire story knowing	facts wise need has
obliged rounds	obliged brother found	population seat equivalent capable
midst begun	nobody assured end	otherwise seeing somewhat Roman
tender need	suddenly genius started	their larger suit knew
dog began	direction woman's press	established suit proposed eyes

Practice Text 7-3 *(continued)*	
5 Words	**6 Words**
bell pray advance pair next	starting star chemistry never associate krill
men occasion they pressed burst	lives fellow fixed showing best protection
among obliged software unless look	anger one extraordinary attention judgment dinner
isn't appeared presently presented however	heart delighted somewhere note brown part
begin sent history always related	talking bug edition love ninety fiduciary
late chapter judge circumstances followed	important eager horses glad pocket husband
can quick help learn madam	computer fly July duke stairs everybody
nose worn six guard all	near repeated described left portion finger
raise success remarkable father's computer	readable composed upon increased release months
beside iron list James principles	below university street progress using event
sudden huge age warranties answer	till justice lose then prince himself
miserable one forces sentence native	month given fit has both expression
slight something Greek other immense	social journey conscience per beg whilst
spite happy pope eternal taste	surrounded come control sand Europe fought
though stars against choose church	violent side assured both general thine
press affairs feelings town me	quarter towards fill ladies faint servant
mere where content coming enjoy	men just joy mere stars box
addressed distant tone finished talked	actually ship pocket several received month
didn't soldiers however readable words	donations never friendship blue surprise night
Egypt thy putting captain honest	error mere where content coming enjoy
however if winter gentleman north	guide consequence threw kings choice vain
naturally manners valley doctor agreed	must add these nice harm valley
dinner between pope surface fortune	drew here Richard inhabitants death drawing

(continued)

Practice Text 7-3 *(continued)*

5 Words	6 Words
dear error pride fill completely	pear terror hide dill effetely snows
wouldn't she's saved dangerous church	will brave write ain't own game
we'll placed you're driven prison	wealth abroad avoid bank drew fast
seek among others social journey	sick sand crowd grant train man
stranger advanced countries main excellent	these relations impression won't colonel anxious
so than bosom of snow	strange conscious sacred sending quarter computer
sign either surely uncle arms	sky surely horse lines excuse rest
blind inside announcement raise character	colonel powerful stage cried affected speaking
fast handsome national supply strange	event unless double guide below march
becoming grand addition fit thirty	audience bread sold welcome junk destroyed
Germany pardon showing Italian deep	girls highest besides wild according cover
Italy thy splendid now home	hide blood related William didn't soldiers
names east girl strange fields	mother's joined sin copyright returned duke
form color honest liberty breath	felt harm midst else clothes eyes
catch throughout heart delighted somewhere	cost Italy younger splendid mind thy
brave write ain't own game	complete Charles wrote center form color
started solemn understanding believed end	that opinion education rage months there
rate rock lifted pray commanded	seeing clicks there desire minds commanded
where angry firm till justice	week proposed forgotten act ready wouldn't
kissed vast ten table repeated	honor circle accept marked self names

Tough, right? You have to pause and consider every word as you read these phrases because they don't make sense — they have no context. You have to read slowly to understand what you're reading. Sometimes you even have to reread and skip backward over the line.

Part III

Advancing Your Speed-Reading Skills

The 5th Wave   By Rich Tennant

EDWARD SCISSORHANDS TAKES UP A HOBBY

"Have you ever tried speed reading without running your finger along the text?"

In this part...

Part III assumes you're aware of the skills you need to be a speed reader, so it presents exercises that reinforce those abilities. Beyond that, it also digs into some refined comprehension skills such as skimming and scanning.

Chapter 8 helps you hone your speed-reading prowess with some challenging exercises. Chapter 9 tells you how to concentrate and read more aggressively, and Chapter 10 looks at skimming, scanning, and prereading, skills useful to anyone who is in a hurry (and who isn't?). In Chapter 11, I show you a couple of high-level skills for advanced speed readers, including how to follow the author's thought patterns and go straight to the gist of the paragraph you're reading.

Chapter 8

Building Your Speed-Reading Momentum

In This Chapter

▶ Reading text in narrow and wide columns

▶ Identifying and reading word groups in the course of your reading

*T*his chapter reinforces basic speed-reading techniques (see Part II). Practice, as they say, makes perfect, so this chapter includes several exercises you can use to hone your speed-reading skills and build momentum before tackling the more advanced techniques described in later chapters. You start with reading text in narrow columns and work your way to reading continuous text that isn't in columns.

To help keep your speed-reading skills on point, revisit the exercises in this chapter (and throughout the book) periodically to check your progress and stay in practice. Head to Chapter 16 for more tidbits on cementing your speed-reading abilities.

Reading Text in Narrow Column Clumps

As Chapter 6 explains, speed reading starts with reading *clumps* — collections of 4 to 16 words that you read in a single glance. A word clump consists of words that are next to each other on the page, nothing more and nothing less. In and of itself, a word clump doesn't have any meaning, unlike word groups and phrases, which do convey meaning. (See Chapter 7 for more on word groups and phrases.)

Exercise 8-1 gives you practice in reading clumps. In the exercise, you read text that has been squeezed — I mean really squeezed — into narrow columns so you have no trouble locating clumps to read. As you read down the columns, take in all the words on each line at once. These word clumps only comprise four or five words at most, so you can read them at once. Bear down with all your concentration to read as fast as you can, keeping in mind that you have to answer comprehension questions when you're done.

Follow these steps to complete Exercise 8-1:

1. **Using a timer, read "Ferdinand Magellan" (Practice Text 8-1), taking in all the words in each line at once as you move down the columns.**

   Keep your eyes fixated in the middle of the column so you can see all the words on each line.

2. **After you finish reading the essay, note in the margin how long you take to read it.**

   You'll want this info for calculating your reading rates in Step 4.

3. **Answer the comprehension questions.**

   You should be able to answer at least four questions correctly. Answer fewer than that and you're sacrificing comprehension for speed.

4. **Calculate your words-per-minute (WPM) rate and effective reading rate (ERR) and enter them on the worksheet in Appendix B.**

   Chapter 5 shows you how to calculate these rates.

Practice Text 8-1

Ferdinand Magellan
Courtesy of www.StrugglingReaders.com

In the early
sixteenth century, a
Portuguese noble, soldier,
and sailor named
Ferdinand Magellan performed
what has been
designated the greatest
single human achievement
on the sea.
Magellan had spent
long years in
Asia, and he
often gazed across
the wide expanse
of the Pacific
Ocean and asked
himself a question:

"How far away
from here are
the lands discovered
by Columbus? If
I sailed to
the New World,
could I find
a passage to
the Pacific Ocean
and the rich
Spice Islands?" Magellan
hoped to find
answers to his
questions as well
as obtain a
large cargo of
rare and costly

spices. When the
Portuguese king refused
to assist him,
he turned to
Spain for help.
On August 10, 1519,
Magellan sailed from
Seville, Spain with
five ships — the
Trinidad, San Antonio,
Concepcion, Victoria, and
Santiago — and a
crew of 237 sailors.
He navigated the
Atlantic, and when
he reached the
New World, he

followed the coast
of South America
until he found
the straits that
connected the two oceans.
He reached this
point on October 21.
It took Magellan
thirty-eight days
to sail through
the stormy straits
to the Pacific
Ocean, and during
that difficult time,
one ship was
wrecked and one
headed back to

Spain. Once in
the waters, which
Magellan named Mar Pacifico
(now the Pacific Ocean)
because of their
apparent stillness, Magellan
turned north and
traveled for months
without sighting land.
The voyage was
filled with extreme
hardship. At one
point several resentful
Spanish captains initiated
a rebellion against
their Portuguese admiral.
Magellan defeated the

(continued)

Practice Text 8-1 *(continued)*

rebels and left two of them on shore to die. Several times the ships ran low on supplies, and the sailors begged to turn back, but Magellan would not allow this. At one point he declared that they would continue the voyage even if they had to eat the leather rigging of the ships.

Disease and starvation claimed many of the crew but, mindful of the fate of the earlier rebels, no one opposed Magellan's will. Magellan finally reached the islands of the Pacific, the Marianas and Guam, in February of 1521, but he was unfortunately killed in a skirmish with some natives in the Philippine Islands on April 27, 1521. The casualties suffered in this battle left the expedition with not enough men to sail the remaining three ships. On May 2, they abandoned the Concepcion and burned the ship. The Basque navigator Juan Sebastian Elcano took over command of the expedition, consisting now only of the ships Trinidad and Victoria.

The crew had over time loaded the two boats with a cargo of valuable spices and at this point an attempt was made to return to Spain by sailing westward. But as they left the Spice Islands, the Trinidad began to take on water. The conclusion was made that the Trinidad needed to spend time in port being repaired, and because the Victoria was not large enough to accommodate all of the surviving crew, only some boarded the ship and sailed for Spain. A few weeks later, the Trinidad, now repaired, departed and attempted to take the same westward route to Spain. However, it was captured by the Portuguese and

Practice Text 8-1 *(continued)*

eventually wrecked while	members in addition	into a Spanish	see the conclusion	he had proved
at anchor under	to Elcano, sailed	port on September 6, 1522,	of the voyage,	what Columbus had
Portuguese control.	west through the	they had been	he and his	correctly predicted, that
The remaining vessel,	Indian Ocean and	gone three years	crew circumnavigated, or	the lands of
the Victoria, with	around the southern	and one month.	sailed around, the	the East could
only 17 of	tip of Africa.	Although Magellan did	world. Magellan would	be reached by
the original crew	When they limped	not live to	never know that	sailing west.

Comprehension Questions

1. What did Magellan hope to find on his journey?

A. Precious metals

B. Lost treasure

C. Rich spices

D. Gun powder

2. How many days did it take Magellan to sail around the straits connecting the Atlantic and Pacific Oceans?

A. 38

B. 54

C. 23

D. 61

3. What did Magellan do to the rebels?

A. Took them back to Spain to be jailed

B. Talked them out of a battle

C. Defeated them and left two on the shore to die

D. Forced them to row his boat as punishment

4. What did Magellan say they would eat before they would turn back?

A. Moldy rice

B. Leather rigging

C. Rotten fish

D. Burnt beans

5. How did Magellan die?

A. His crew threw him overboard.

B. He went down with the ship.

C. He did of old age.

D. He was killed in a battle with some natives.

Answer key: 1. C; **2.** A; **3.** C; **4.** B; **5.** D

Reading Clump Text in Wider Columns

As a beginning speed reader, you can only read four- and five-word clumps, but with practice doing exercises like Exercise 8-2, you can soon jump to six-, seven-, eight-, and even nine- and ten-word clumps.

Exercise 8-2 stretches your horizontal reading vision a little. In this exercise, you read an essay laid out in two wide columns and answer some comprehension questions. Each column contains anywhere from five to eight words. In this exercise, I want you to treat those five to eight words as a clump and read them in one gulp.

To knock out Exercise 8-2, complete the following steps:

1. **Using a timer, read "Obstacles Are the Stepping Stones of Success" (Practice Text 8-2), trying to take in the words in each line with a single glance.**

   On each line, focus your eyes on the middle of the column and take in all the words to the left and right.

2. **When you finish reading the essay, note in the margin how long you take to read it.**

   You'll want this info for calculating your reading rates in Step 4.

3. **Answer the comprehension questions.**

   If you're comprehending what you read as well as speed reading the words, you should be able to answer at least four of the five questions.

4. **On the worksheet in Appendix B, enter your WPM rate and ERR (see Chapter 5 for these formulas).**

Practice Text 8-2

Obstacles Are the Stepping Stones of Success
by Harvey Mackay, nationally syndicated columnist
Originally published October 28, 2001

A man was walking in the park

one day when he came upon

a cocoon with a small opening.

He sat and watched the butterfly

for several hours as it struggled

to force its body through the little hole.

Then it seemed to stop making any progress.

It looked like it had gotten

as far as it could,

so the man decided to help the butterfly.

He used his pocketknife and snipped

the remaining bit of the cocoon.

The butterfly then emerged easily, but

something was strange. The butterfly

had a swollen body and shriveled wings.

The man continued to watch the butterfly

because he expected at any moment

the wings would enlarge and expand

to be able to support the body,

which would contract in time.

Neither happened. In fact, the butterfly

spent the rest of its life crawling around

with a swollen body and deformed wings.

It was never able to fly.

What the man in his kindness and haste

did not understand was that

Practice Text 8-2 *(continued)*

the restricting cocoon and the struggle

required for the butterfly to emerge was natural.

It was nature's way of forcing fluid

from its body into its wings

so that it would be ready for flight

once it achieved its freedom.

Sometimes struggles are exactly what

we need in our lives.

If we were allowed to go through life

without any obstacles, we would be crippled.

We would not be as strong as

what we could have been.

And we could never fly.

History has shown us that

the most celebrated winners usually

encountered heartbreaking obstacles before they triumphed.

They won because they refused

to become discouraged by their defeats.

My good friend, Lou Holtz,

football coach of the University of South Carolina,

once told me, "Show me someone who

has done something worthwhile, and I'll show you

someone who has overcome adversity."

Beethoven composed his greatest works after becoming deaf.

George Washington was snowed in

through a treacherous winter at Valley Forge.

Abraham Lincoln was raised in poverty.

Albert Einstein was called a

slow learner, retarded and uneducable.

If Christopher Columbus had turned back,

(continued)

Practice Text 8-2 (continued)

no one could have blamed him,

considering the constant adversity he endured.

As an elementary student, actor

James Earl Jones (a.k.a. Darth Vader)

stuttered so badly he communicated

with friends and teachers using written notes.

Itzhak Perlman, the incomparable concert violinist,

was born to parents who survived

a Nazi concentration camp and

has been paralyzed from the

waist down since the age of four.

Chester Carlson, a young inventor, took his idea

to 20 big corporations in the 1940s.

After seven years of rejections,

he was able to persuade Haloid,

a small company in Rochester, N.Y.,

to purchase the rights to

his electrostatic paper-copying process.

Haloid has since become Xerox Corporation.

Thomas Edison tried over 2,000 experiments

before he was able to

get his light bulb to work.

Upon being asked how he felt

about failing so many times, he replied,

"I never failed once. I invented the light bulb.

It just happened to be a 2,000-step process."

Franklin Delano Roosevelt, elected President of the United States

for four terms, had been stricken

with polio at the age of 39.

Persistence paid off for General Douglas MacArthur.

Practice Text 8-2 *(continued)*

After applying for admission to West Point twice,

he applied a third time

and was accepted. The rest is history.

In 1927 the head instructor of the

John Murray Anderson Drama School,

instructed student Lucille Ball

to "Try any other profession. Any other."

Buddy Holly was fired from the

Decca record label in 1956 by Paul Cohen,

Nashville "Artists and Repertoire Man."

Cohen called Holly "the biggest

no-talent I ever worked with."

Academy Award-winning writer, producer and director

Woody Allen failed motion picture production

at New York University (NYU)

and City College of New York.

He also flunked English at NYU.

Helen Keller, the famous blind author and speaker,

said: "Character cannot be developed

in ease and quiet. Only through experience

of trial and suffering can the

soul be strengthened, vision cleared,

ambition inspired and success achieved.

Silver is purified in fire

and so are we. It is in

the most trying times that

our real character is shaped and revealed."

Mackay's Moral: There is no education

like the university of adversity.

Comprehension Questions

1. **What are the stepping stones of success?**

   A. Obstacles

   B. Good friends

   C. Family

   D. Character traits

2. **Who flunked English in college?**

   A. Helen Keller

   B. Buddy Holly

   C. Woody Allen

   D. Franklin Delano Roosevelt

3. **Who was called "a slow-learner, retarded and unedu-cable??**

   A. Albert Einstein

   B. James Earl Jones

   C. Helen Keller

   D. Thomas Edison

4. **Who stuttered badly as an elementary student?**

   A. Helen Keller

   B. Woody Allen

   C. Thomas Edison

   D. James Earl Jones

5. **Who was told to "try another profession"?**

   A. Woody Allen

   B. Lucille Ball

   C. James Earl Jones

   D. Franklin Delano Roosevelt

Answer key: 1: A; **2:** C; **3:** A; **4:** D; **5:** B

Identifying Word Groups in Continuous Text

Chapter 7 details how a *word group* is basically a sophisticated clump. Where a clump is just several words run together on the page, a word group is a phrase or thought that carries meaning. If you can master the art of recognizing word groups as you read and read each word group in one go, you can become a much faster reader.

The purpose of Exercise 8-3 is to help you get in the habit of seeing word groups as you read continuous text. (If you haven't already taken a look at Chapters 7 and 11, you may want to check out their discussions on recognizing word groups, phrases, and thought groups before doing this exercise.) In the exercise, you underline word groups so you can get practice in identifying them. You also answer five comprehension questions to make sure you understand what you read instead of just flying through it.

Note: Obviously, the fact that you carefully review the practice text in the course of underlining will help improve your reading speed as well; after all, you will have already read it to some extent once before you officially read it for speed. However, that little bit of extra familiarity isn't enough to improve your speed as much as reading for word groups does. So grab a pencil and dive into Exercise 8-3 (although maybe you'd better step lightly instead; you *are* holding a pencil):

1. **Read the essay "Culture" (Practice Text 8-3), underlining the word groups as you read.**

   To help you get started, I've underlined the word groups in the first paragraph of the essay. Don't worry about whether you underline the right word; there's no strict definition of what constitutes a word group. The point is to get in the habit of seeing and recognizing words groups in the course of your reading.

2. **When you finish underlining the word groups, get out your timer and read the essay word group by word group.**

   You underlined the word groups, so you shouldn't have any trouble finding them. Read each underlined word group in a single glance if you can.

3. **After you finish reading the essay, jot down your reading time in the margin.**

   This info helps you calculate your reading rates in Step 5.

4. Answer the comprehension questions.

You should be able to answer at least four of five questions correctly if you're reading for comprehension as well as speed.

5. In the Appendix B worksheet, enter your WPM rate and ERR for Exercise 8-3.

The better you are at recognizing word groups in the course of your reading, the faster you can read.

Practice Text 8-3

Culture
Courtesy of www.StrugglingReaders.com

When you think of a culture, you usually think of things such as art, language, music, literature, and architecture. But a culture is much more. It is a way of life, simple or complex.

Every society or group of people has a culture. The culture includes a mixture of art, language, music, literature, and architecture. But it also includes customs, traditions, and beliefs that are important to the groups within families, neighborhoods, communities, and governments.

Cultures result from basic needs shared by all people. Early culture was a way to extend the ability to obtain food, seek protection, and raise and nurture children. Today's culture has modern methods of getting food and developing shelter. It has a means of distributing the food and other goods to its people. The culture includes family relationships, community relationships, education opportunities, religious practices, and forms of artistic expression.

All large cities and many small cities have history, science, and art centers, and museums. People attend dance performances, plays, musicals, and classical and popular music concerts. They can view outdoor art projects and important architecture. This development of artistic expression forms is the result of both contributions by private giving and other funding.

A country's culture has systems for giving power and responsibility, including social positions, education, economics, and governments. Giving power and responsibility is a way to keep order and settle disputes.

Practice Text 8-3 *(continued)*

In more complex cultures, this includes police, court, and prison systems. The country's structure, its laws, and the way people relate to each other have great influence on people's actions and attitudes.

People learn their culture by growing up in a particular society or group. They are not born with a culture. They learn it mainly through the use of language and by watching and imitating other group members. By seeing what goes on around then, they learn what their society considers right and wrong.

By listening to group members' shared memories, beliefs, values, and expectations, they develop ways of thinking. Most cultural learning comes from verbal communication. Children share their culture's traditions of citizenship, holiday celebration, craftsmanship, production, competition, leadership, know-how, and positive attitude.

To learn about a group's culture, ask questions as "What languages do the group's members speak? How do group members decide what is right or wrong? What customs do group members share?"

Customs are an important feature of a culture — they're a way of doing things that has been handed down from one generation to the next. Customs include greeting traditions, eating traditions, and holiday traditions. Every culture has a customary way of greeting, of eating, and of celebrating holidays and special days. The adventure of fireworks displays on the Fourth of July has become an American custom.

Through travel, television, films, and other means, people become familiar with cultures from around the world. And cultural traits spread around the world. Clothing, music, sports, and industrial processes are the same in many places of the world.

Blue jeans are a good example of a spreading cultural trait. Clothing from one culture, American, is worn around the world. Blue jeans became popular as work clothes in the 1850s after Levi Strauss, a German immigrant merchant in San Francisco, created them. Now they are widely worn on every continent by people of all ages and fashion tastes.

A culture is much more than art, language, music, literature, and architecture. It is a way to enhance the lives of people.

Comprehension Questions

1. Most cultural learning comes from _____ communication.

   A. Verbal

   B. Aural

   C. Visual

   D. Physical

2. _____ are a way of doing things that has been handed down through generations.

   A. Habits

   B. Customs

   C. Behaviors

   D. Repetitions

3. Culture includes all of the following except

   A. Family relationships

   B. Community relationships

   C. Psychological relationships

   D. Religious practices

4. Culture results from basic _____ shared by all people.

   A. Desires

   B. Needs

   C. Habits

   D. Thoughts

5. Blue jeans were invented by Levi Strauss, a German immigrant who lived in

   A. Los Angeles

   B. Chicago

   C. New York

   D. San Francisco

Answer key: 1. A; **2.** B; **3.** C; **4.** B; **5.** D

Reading Word Groups in Continuous Text

Exercise 8-4 challenges you to recognize and identify word groups in the course of your reading. As each word group appears before your eyes, you see it, read it, and comprehend it. With a bit of practice you can become adept at seeing word groups in text in the same way that you see different colors in a painting.

Unlike Exercise 8-3 in the previous section, you don't identify the word groups ahead of time; you do it as you read. Developing the ability to see and comprehend word groups on the fly helps you become a better speed reader. Follow these steps to complete Exercise 8-4, keeping in mind that you answer comprehension questions at the end:

1. **Using a timer, read "Psychology" (Practice Text 8-4) word group by word group.**

   Do your very best to read word group by word group, not clump by clump (and especially not word by word). If you focus hard enough, the word groups will stick out, and you'll be able to identify them.

2. **Write down in the margin how long you take to read the essay.**

   Your reading time helps determine your reading rates in Step 4.

3. **Answer the comprehension questions.**

   As long as you're not sacrificing speed for comprehension, you should be able to answer at least four questions correctly.

4. **In Appendix B, enter your WPM rate and ERR for Exercise 8-4.**

Practice Text 8-4

Psychology
Courtesy of www.StrugglingReaders.com

Psychology is the scientific study of behavior and the mind. It is a popular subject with many fascinating features.

The word *psychology* comes from the Greek words *psyche,* meaning mind or soul, and *logia,* meaning study. Since ancient times, people have been interested in why human beings and

(continued)

Practice Text 8-4 (continued)

---

other animals behave as they do. The origins of psychology are often traced to the ancient Greek philosopher Aristotle, whose main interest was in what the human mind can accomplish.

Psychologists seek answers to a wide range of human behaviors such as: How do our brains learn and remember? How does the mind affect the body? (One answer for this behavior is that some people are able to change their heart rates and body temperatures just by thinking about doing so.) What about personality differences in people? Why are some people bashful and some not shy at all? What causes violence? How can violence be stopped?

Psychological research is applied to a wide range of human activity related to everyday life, such as family, education, employment, and mental health. Psychology is a broad and diverse field and includes areas such as human development, cognitive development (the mental processing of information), and others. More than any other part of the human body, the brain raises questions that psychologists are searching to answer.

A number of different specialty areas in psychology have emerged. One of these is sports psychology, which deals with increasing athletic performance A sport psychologist may work with individual athletes or team athletes to improve performance levels. Some of the most important skills taught are goal setting, relaxation, visualization, awareness and control, concentration, and confidence.

Some sport psychologists also work in the fitness industry to design exercise programs that enhance participation and promote psychological well-being.

Psychologists use scientific methods to test their ideas. Three methods are often used in psychological research.

The first method is naturalistic observation, observing the behavior of human beings and other animals in their natural environments. Here is an example of naturalistic observation. The study of parent-child interaction may involve videotaping the parent and child in their home either as they go about their daily routine or as they perform an activity given to them by the researcher. The videotaped interactions can then be analyzed to learn information from them.

The second method is systematic assessment that identifies and examines people's thoughts, feelings, and personality traits with case histories, surveys and standardized tests. Things such as intelligence and reading ability can be measured through standardized tests.

Practice Text 8-4 *(continued)*

The third method uses experimentation to discover or confirm cause and effect relationships. It enables a scientist to test a theory under controlled conditions. To demonstrate a cause and effect, an experiment must often show that, for example, if something occurs after a certain treatment is given to a subject, the same thing should *not* occur in the *absence* of the treatment.

Psychology is closely related to the natural science of biology and the social sciences of sociology and anthropology that deal with people in society. Social sciences study the attitudes and relationships of human beings in social settings. Psychology is similar to a medical field called psychiatry; however, psychiatrists have medical degrees and usually focus on treating mental disorders.

Research findings in psychology have greatly increased the possibility of understanding why people behave as they do. They have provided valuable insights into helping people function better individually and as a group or society. Psychological research and experimentation are fascinating, but how people actually benefit from the findings is the true measure of success.

Comprehension Questions

1. Psychology is the scientific study of

    A. The behavior of the mind

    B. Climate conditions

    C. The body's major organs

    D. Blood

2. The word *psyche* means

    A. Thinking

    B. Mind and soul

    C. Head

    D. Brains

3. *Logia* means

    A. Behaviors

    B. Experiment

    C. Test

    D. Study

4. The origins of psychology can be traced back to ancient

    A. Rome

    B. Turkey

    C. Greece

    D. Egypt

5. Aristotle's main interest was in

    A. Discovering the cause of mental disorders

    B. Studying mathematics

    C. What the human mind can accomplish

    D. Architecture

Answer key: 1. A; **2.** B; **3.** D; **4.** C; **5.** C

Chapter 9

Exercising Your Ability to Read More in Even Less Time

In This Chapter

▶ Keeping vocalization to a minimum

▶ Expanding your reading vision

▶ Reading with heightened concentration

▶ Reading aggressively

*T*his chapter puts you to the test by presenting four unique speed-reading exercises designed to help you hone your speed-reading skills: avoiding vocalizing, expanding your vision span, concentrating harder, and reading aggressively.

Introducing Push-Down and Push-Up Exercises

My company, The Literacy Company, created *push-down* and *push-up exercises* to reinforce essential speed-reading skills.

✔ **Push-down exercises:** You read the same material multiple times, trying to read the same amount of material in less time each go-around. After each reading, you also answer who, what, where, and when questions, which demonstrate how comprehension, retention, and recall improve at each subsequent reading. (And there's nothing like the threat — I mean promise — of a quiz to encourage you to pay attention to the material instead of speed-skimming it.)

✔ **Push-up exercises:** You read the same material multiple times for the same amount of time, trying to read farther and farther in that allotted time each go-around. This exercise demonstrates how the familiarity with text and vocabulary increases reading speed.

Push-down and push-up exercises really challenge you to bear down and apply all your speed-reading skills. They also give you a chance to realistically measure how much faster you can read if you put your heart and mind into it.

Getting More from What You Read: Push-Down Exercises

The exercises in this section are designed to reinforce two essential speed-reading skills: not vocalizing and expanding your vision span. I would argue that these are actually the two most essential speed-reading skills. Master these two skills and you are well on your way to becoming a speed reader.

Focusing on your silent reading

The first goal of anybody who wants to be a speed reader is to cut down or eliminate *vocalization* (the bad habit of saying and hearing words when you read — check out Chapter 2 for more). Vocalizing keeps you from reading fast because it takes much longer to see, hear, and process words than it takes to just see and process them.

In Exercise 9-1, you read an essay called "The Incredible Brain" twice. As you read, try to read in complete silence without your inner voice making a peep.

You may even try reading this essay while chewing gum or with a pencil between your lips. Keeping your mouth and lips busy while you read can help stifle, perhaps even silence, your inner reading voice.

Follow these steps to complete the first half of Exercise 9-1:

1. **Using a timer, read as much of "The Incredible Brain" (Practice Text 9-1) as you can in 60 seconds (remembering not to vocalize as you read).**

   If you hear your inner reading voice, imagine a volume switch next to your right ear and turn the volume all the way down.

2. **When the 60 seconds have elapsed, circle the last word you read.**

3. **On the worksheet in Appendix B, write down the line number of the circled word.**

   For example, if the word you circled is in line 35, enter 35 on the Appendix B worksheet.

Practice Text 9-1

The Incredible Brain
Courtesy of www.StrugglingReaders.com

Human beings have the most highly developed brains of any living creatures. More powerful than the most advanced super-computer, the human brain makes it possible for a person to live, speak, solve problems, make and enjoy music, and create
5 through thoughts and ideas.

The brain is the body's control center. It constantly receives information about conditions both inside and outside the body. It rapidly analyzes the information and then sends out messages that control bodily functions and actions.

10 Three main parts or areas make up the brain: brain stem, cer-ebellum, and cerebrum. The brain stem is at the bottom of the brain and controls the body's automatic processes, such as breathing, heartbeat, and body temperature. The cerebellum lies at the back of the brain. It is the part of the brain that coor-
15 dinates balance, posture, and movements. The cerebrum is the center of all thought and includes about 90 percent of the human brain.

The cerebrum is divided into two halves called hemispheres. Each hemisphere is responsible for specific functions. In
20 general, the left cerebral hemisphere is involved with mathe-matics, language, and logical thinking. The right cerebral hemi-sphere includes feelings, musical ability, and visual thinking. While each hemisphere has specific functions, the two hemi-spheres are thought to also process information together. For
25 example, while the left hemisphere processes the meanings of words, the right hemisphere processes the emotions related to the words. In most human beings that are right handed, it is the left hemisphere that usually contains the specialized lan-guage areas. About 20 percent of left-handed people have their
30 language areas in the right hemisphere.

The human brain is a gray-colored organ. Its jelly-like mass has many grooves and ridges on its surface. An infant's brain weighs less than one pound. By the time a child is six years old, the brain has reached its full weight of approximately
35 three pounds. During the six-year growth period, a child learns and acquires information at the fastest rate in his or her life.

Although the brain reaches its full weight by six years old, some parts of the brain do not fully develop until after the teenage years. An environment that stimulates learning actu-
40 ally builds important networks in the brains of young learners.

(continued)

Practice Text 9-1 *(continued)*

It was once believed that as one aged, the brain's networks became fixed, like plastic hardening. In the past twenty years, however, an enormous amount of research has revealed that the brain never stops changing and adjusting. Therefore,
45 throughout life, while reading, studying, and learning, new brain networks are being built.

Proper brain development and functioning also depend on good nutrition. Eating a good diet and drinking adequate water is important for brain development and function. The brain is
50 about 80 percent water. Even slight dehydration can damage the brain over time. Exercise is also important for brain development and functioning.

The brain works like a computer and a chemical factory. Brain cells produce electrical signals and send them from cell to cell along pathways called circuits. As in a computer, these cir-
55 cuits receive, process, store, and retrieve information. Unlike a computer, the brain creates its electrical signals by chemical means. The brain depends on many complicated chemical substances working together simultaneously.

60 Among the many interesting facts about the human brain are that the brain does not feel pain because it has no pain receptors and that women have about ten percent more of the brain cells called neurons than men do.

Human brains are the most highly developed brains, more
65 powerful than computers. Research continues to discover amazing information about the incredible human brain.

In the second half of Exercise 9-1, I ask you to answer some comprehension questions. Although I want you to read fast, don't sacrifice comprehension for speed. Follow these steps to complete the second half of Exercise 9-1:

1. **Using a timer, start reading the essay again, and read as far as you can in 50 seconds, striving to get at least to the same line you got to previously.**

   Double your efforts to read silently. You'll likely read faster this time because you've already read most of this essay and you're familiar with the subject matter, but if you don't read faster, don't blame yourself. Blame the clock — it always ticks faster when you're trying to go faster.

2. **Draw a square around the last word you read when the 50 seconds expire and record the line number in Appendix B.**

3. Answer the following comprehension questions.

I want you to answer the comprehension questions to make sure you're reading for comprehension as well as speed. You should be able to answer four out of five questions correctly. If your score is lower than that, focus more on concentration in your next reading test. Pretend that the reading test is the only thing in the world that matters and really bear down when you read.

Comprehension Questions

1. The human brain is commonly known as

    A. The most important organ

    B. The body's information highway

    C. A supercomputer

    D. The body's control center

2. Which of the following is not controlled by the brain stem?

    A. Body temperature

    B. Language

    C. Heartbeat

    D. Breathing

3. Which part of the brain is responsible for balance, posture, and the coordination of movements?

    A. The cerebellum

    B. The brain stem

    C. The cerebrum

    D. The cortex

4. The largest part of the brain is called the

    A. Brain stem

    B. Cerebellum

    C. Cerebrum

    D. Frontal lobe

5. How much does an adult brain weigh?

    A. 1 pound

    B. 3 pounds

    C. 5 pounds

    D. 7 pounds

Answer key: 1. D; **2.** B; **3.** A; **4.** C; **5.** B

Spreading your vision span even wider

Another key to being a speed reader is to widen your *vision span,* or how many words you take in at a time. As you read, your eyes move across the page, fixating on single words or groups of words. To improve your reading speed, you need to take in more words with each glance or *eye fixation* (check out Chapter 3 for more on eye fixations). Exercise 9-2 builds on the exercise in the previous section by training you to use a widened vision span to reach your reading goals in less time.

In Exercise 9-2, you read an essay called "Lewis and Clark" twice. Focus on reading more than one word at a time. (For more information on taking in multiple words in one glance, check out the Chapter 6 discussion on reading word clumps and the Chapter 7 discussion about recognizing and reading word groups with a single eye fixation.)

Follow these steps to complete the first half of Exercise 9-2:

1. **Using a timer, read "Lewis and Clark" (Practice Text 9-2) for 60 seconds, trying to take in word groups in a single glance.**

   For example, the first words in the essay, "In April 1803, President Thomas Jefferson," are a word group. You can read much more quickly if you take in word groups like this with a single eye fixation.

2. **When the 60 seconds have passed, circle the last word you read and record its line number on the worksheet in Appendix B.**

Practice Text 9-2

Lewis and Clark
Courtesy of www.StrugglingReaders.com

    In April 1803, President Thomas Jefferson purchased the entire area of Louisiana from France. The territory stretched from the Mississippi River to the middle of the Rocky Mountains, but no one was really sure where the Mississippi River started
5 or where exactly the Rocky Mountains were located. In June of 1803, Meriwether Lewis was commissioned by Jefferson to find answers to some of the many questions that people had regarding the new purchase. Captain Lewis selected William Clark as his partner in the exploration. They were to explore
10 the area and describe the land and its human and animal inhabitants.

Practice Text 9-2 *(continued)*

During the winter of 1803-1804, recruitment and training were undertaken at Camp Dubois, Illinois Territory. Located near present-day Hartford, Illinois, Camp Dubois was the begin-
15 ning point of the journey, where, on May 14, 1804, Lewis and Clark departed with 33 men who comprised the "Permanent Party" of the expedition and sufficient supplies for two years. Supplies included a ton of dried pork, seven buckets of salt, and medicines for all the men of the expedition. They paddled
20 up the Missouri River in canoes and met with Lewis in Saint Charles, Missouri.

The expedition continued up the Missouri westward and met and traded with a variety of Native American tribes. In August of 1804, the Corps of Discovery, the official name of the expedi-
25 tion, suffered its only death when Sergeant Charles Floyd died of acute appendicitis. With the coming of winter, the party built Fort Mandan near Washburn, North Dakota. It was here that they became acquainted with a sixteen-year-old Indian woman and adopted her as their primary guide. Her name was
30 Sacagawea, which means "bird woman." She was the wife of a French-Canadian fur trapper named Toussaint Charbonneau that Lewis And Clark employed during their winter stay at Fort Mandan.

When the ice melted, they continued on their journey. All
35 along the way, Lewis and Clark drew maps and diagrams and recorded what they observed in meticulous detail. They encountered Native American leaders, told them about the United States, and presented them with medals and American flags from the president. They acquired knowledge about soil
40 and weather conditions and investigated fur trading possibili-
ties. After seven months of difficult travel, they reached the Rocky Mountains.

Thanks to Sacagawea's influence, Lewis and Clark obtained horses from the Native Americans. Their intention was to
45 cross the Rockies with the Pacific Ocean as their final destina-
tion. The weather grew cold, the food became scarce, and the mountains seemed endless.

When they finally arrived at the ocean in December of 1805, Clark wrote in his journal, "The ocean is in view! Oh, what joy!"
50 The expedition spent the winter at Fort Caltsop, which they built to prepare provisions for their trip home. They hunted wildlife, spent time with more of the over 36 tribes that they would encounter during their more than two-year journey.

(continued)

Practice Text 9-2 *(continued)*

When the expedition finally returned home over two years
55 and four months after they began their journey, they were
awarded a tumultuous welcome. People had long since given
them up for dead. That welcome was well deserved. During the
long and arduous voyage, Lewis and Clark had accomplished
an outstanding feat in describing the land, the rivers, and the
60 Native American inhabitants.

Their perception of the geography of the Northwest allowed
them to fill in details of previously unknown areas of the north-
western United States. They prepared nearly 140 maps during
the entire journey. Their trip also documented over 100 spe-
65 cies of animals and nearly 176 species of native plants. Their
contribution to the knowledge of this area was incalculable.
They had proven that there was a way to reach the Pacific and
had opened a huge new area for settlement and trade. Many
other Americans would soon follow in their footsteps.

Heads up: In the second half of Exercise 9-2, I ask you to answer
some comprehension questions, so read for meaning as well as
speed. The following steps show you how to complete the second
half of Exercise 9-2:

1. **Using your timer, read the essay again, reading as far as
   you can in 50 seconds with the goal of reaching at least
   your previous stopping point.**

   On this reading, you're more aware of word groups
   because you read the essay already.

2. **Draw a square around the last word you read when the
   50 seconds expired and enter its line number in the
   Appendix B worksheet.**

   If you didn't make it past your previous stopping point,
   don't sweat it. Just try harder next time. In speed reading,
   you always have to try, try, try again.

3. **Answer the following comprehension questions.**

   You should be able to answer four out of five questions
   correctly. If you score lower than that, work on your comprehension as well as your reading speed. You may have to
   slow down a bit to improve your comprehension, but that's
   okay. Comprehension is the goal of any reading activity,
   isn't it?

Comprehension Questions

1. **Which U.S. president purchased the entire area of Louisiana from France?**

   A. John Adams

   B. John Madison

   C. Thomas Jefferson

   D. John Quincy Adams

2. **Why did Jefferson ask Meriwether Lewis and William Clark to explore the area and describe the land and its human and animal inhabitants?**

   A. France did not give the American government all of the information about the purchased are that it had in its files.

   B. The U.S. did not want to pay for the land without a survey.

   C. It was just a formality necessary to close the transaction.

   D. No one, neither American nor French, knew much about the land that France sold America.

3. **How long did Lewis and Clark think it would take to survey the Louisiana Purchase?**

   A. 6 months

   B. 2 years

   C. 1 month

   D. 10 months

4. **What was the name of the woman they took as their guide?**

   A. Sacagawea

   B. So Kim

   C. Tohono O'Odham

   D. Alice

5. **What was one of the main accomplishments of the Lewis and Clark expedition?**

   A. They acquired knowledge of the soil and weather.

   B. They reached the Pacific Ocean.

   C. They reached the Rocky Mountains.

   D. They acquired knowledge about the animals that lived in the Louisiana Territory.

Answer key: 1. C; **2.** D; **3.** B; **4.** A; **5.** B

Advancing Your Reading Limit: Push-Up Exercises

The exercises in this section reinforce two essential speed-reading skills: concentrating harder and reading aggressively. Speed reading is more than a set of techniques — it's also a mindset. You plunge ahead, confident that you can read quickly and comprehend at a heightened speed. These exercises help put you in that speed-reading mindset.

Reading aggressively without regressing

Above and beyond technique, speed reading is a state of mind in which you read more aggressively. Speed readers gallop across the page; they're confident readers who forge ahead without *regressing*, or going back over the material to check understanding. (Head to Chapter 2 for more on regression.) When you do the exercises in this section, I want you to flex your reading muscles. I want you to see whether you can adopt the aggressive reading mindset.

Reading aggressively takes work — it can be fatiguing. But you have to build up your stamina and be an aggressive reader if you really want to increase your reading speed.

Exercise 9-3 helps you become a more aggressive reader. Read the essay "Volunteerism: You Often Receive More than You Give" three times. On each subsequent reading, try to read more words than you did the time before — try to read more aggressively.

Follow these steps to complete the first half of Exercise 9-3:

1. **Using a timer, read as much of the essay "Volunteerism: You Often Receive More than You Give" (Practice Text 9-3) in your normal reading mode as you can in 60 seconds.**

2. **Circle the last word you read when the 60 seconds expire and note its line number.**

3. **Reset the timer for 60 seconds and reread the essay aggressively, trying to read farther than you did in Step 1.**

   Read as if your life depends on it.

Practice Text 9-3

Volunteerism: You Often Receive More than You Give
by Harvey Mackay, nationally syndicated columnist
Originally published June 17, 2006

You don't have to pledge Skull and Bones or be a country club deb to meet the right people. There are a ton of jobs that offer that opportunity but go begging every year for want of volunteers willing to take them.

5 Take ushering at your church or synagogue. Maybe it sounds like it's just one step ahead of stoking the boilers, but it's one of the most important jobs around the place. It only takes an hour a week, and there's no heavy lifting. You can look on it as a "poor man's finishing school." It will help you overcome
10 any innate shyness you may have about meeting and greeting strangers, and if you do it properly, you'll really enjoy it.

Smart leaders of growing congregations make sure they have an ushering crew that stands tall. The ushers set the tone. Is it a friendly place with a warm welcome or an ingrown deal with
15 very little to offer newcomers?

The Reverend James Kennedy, pastor of the well-known Coral Ridge Presbyterian Church in Fort Lauderdale, has a church that attracts a tremendous number of visitors. The ushers at Coral Ridge are instructed to be certain everyone is welcomed
20 by at least two or three people and told they "were glad you came to worship with us today." The church benefits greatly from these volunteers, but so do the individual ushers who become polished ambassadors for their congregation.

Getting active in an organization can help you in areas where
25 you may be weak. Afraid to speak in front of a group? You won't be toast if you join Toastmasters. I did, and I can tell you that the basics I learned in this organization are the primary reasons for any success I've had as a public speaker.

Also, Toastmasters helps you develop:

30 • self-esteem,

• assertiveness,

• confidence, and

• leadership.

Because volunteerism almost always includes fund-raising, you
35 have an unusual opportunity to hone your selling skills. You will get a ton of no's but what better way to receive on-the-job training than on someone else's payroll.

(continued)

Practice Text 9-3 *(continued)*

When you do volunteer work, you can learn how to run a meeting, prepare reports, serve on committees, supervise others, and
40 a thousand other skills that can help you in your own career. Sometimes, it's impossible to learn these things on the job.

Most of the people who sign up for these volunteer chores stay active for decades. Here's an opportunity to learn teamwork and have the satisfaction of providing a vital service. You'll
45 make new friends, and you'll be able to develop other contacts within the community itself.

Sometimes the rewards of volunteering are unexpected.

Will was a pretty fair high school athlete, but he dropped out of college before he could make any mark in athletics. He loved
50 hockey and despite a career of mostly lower level blue collar jobs, he found enough time to coach kid hockey teams. Most of his friends thought he was crazy to spend so much time coaching for nothing when he didn't have two quarters to rub together.

55 However, one of the contacts he made with his coaching really paid off, and today Will has a job he never dreamed he could get . . . sales manager for a well-respected paper company.

Sometimes, the only rewards for volunteering are the satisfaction of doing a thankless job well. But sometimes, there is a
60 personal payoff, and it can come in surprising ways.

Follow these steps to complete the second half of Exercise 9-3:

1. **Reset the timer for 60 seconds and reread the essay aggressively, trying to read farther than you did previously.**

   Read as if your life depended on it.

2. **Draw a square around the last word you read when the 60 seconds expired and note its line number.**

   Did you read farther? Significantly farther? If you didn't, think about how you can read more aggressively in the future. Try to focus harder when you read and make this your primary speed-reading goal.

3. **Repeat Steps 1 and 2, attacking the essay a third time and drawing a triangle around the last word you read.**

   I suspect you were able to read more words on each subsequent reading.

4. Answer the following comprehension questions.

You should be able to answer four out of the five questions correctly. A lower score suggests that you've forfeited comprehension for speed. Focus more on your comprehension in your future reading.

Comprehension Questions

1. Who is the pastor of the Coral Ridge Presbyterian Church?

A. John Kennedy

B. James Kennedy

C. Joseph Kennedy

D. Jay Kennedy

2. Where is the Coral Ridge Presbyterian Church?

A. Fort Lauderdale

B. Miami

C. Dade

D. Coral Ridge

3. In what group did Harvey Mackay learn many of his public speaking skills?

A. Toastmasters

B. Toasters

C. Toastmakers

D. Toasties

4. What's the name of the man in the article who coached kids' hockey?

A. Bill

B. William

C. Billy

D. Will

5. What kind of job did the kids' hockey coach get through one of the contacts made there?

A. Newspaper writer

B. Volunteer

C. Sales Manager

D. Salesman

Answer key: 1: B; **2:** A; **3:** A; **4:** D; **5:** C

Improving your concentration

In many ways, speed reading is just the act of reading with a deeper level of concentration and efficiency. You have to concentrate harder when you speed read because you do several things at once in the act of speed reading:

- ✔ You consciously try to read several words at the same time.
- ✔ You try to detect and read word groups with a single eye fixation.
- ✔ You do your best to keep from vocalizing.

Exercise 9-4 is designed to help you be aware of how well you concentrate when you speed read by requiring you to read an essay multiple times with ever-increasing degrees of concentration.

Follow these steps to complete the first half of Exercise 9-4:

1. **Using a timer, read as much of the essay "Transportation" (Practice Text 9-4) as you can in 60 seconds.**

   Bear down and really concentrate on the words. Pretend that the essay is the only thing in the world and it deserves all of your attention.

2. **Circle the last word you read when the 60 seconds elapsed, and note its line number.**

   In your next reading, you try to read 25 percent more text in the allotted minute.

3. **Calculate what line you have to reach to read 25 percent more text, and draw a square around that line.**

   Divide the line number you circled in Step 2 by four and then add that result to the circled line number. For example, if you read to line 60, you take 60 ÷ 4 (which equals 15) and then add 15 to the original 60 to get your new goal of 75 lines. You can round up or down if you end up with a decimal target (like line 66.25).

   If you have decent math skills or a handy calculator, just multiply the Step 2 line number by 1.25 to quickly determine your new goal line.

Practice Text 9-4

Transportation
Courtesy of www.StrugglingReaders.com

Transportation, the act of carrying people and goods from one place to another, has made great gains since early civilization.

In early civilization, transportation developed slowly. Throughout most of the prehistoric period, people traveled
5   mainly on foot. They had no wheeled vehicles or roads. Some scientists believe that wheeled carts appeared around 3500 B.C. in Mesopotamia, a region of the Middle East. As civilizations developed, the need for better forms of transportation grew.

Water transportation in the form of ships and barges devel-
10   oped more quickly than land transportation. Most of the world's trade was by sea. In the 1700s, the first practical steam engine was invented. This led to the steamship, and in the 1820s, to railroad transportation.

In the 1860s, the railroad expanded quickly across the United
15   States to serve industries and growing cities. As part of the industrialization of the United States, a vast network of railroads connected the United States from coast to coast. This was the transcontinental rail system, for the transport of
20   people and goods.

The evolution of modern land transportation began in Europe and the United States in the late 1800s with the introduction of electric trains and streetcars. Then two inventions led to modern automobiles: the pneumatic, air-filled tire and the internal combustion engine. At first few people could afford automobiles;
25   however, during the 1920s, mass production of automobiles on assembly lines made them affordable to a greater segment of the population. Automobiles became the chief means of passenger transportation in the United States during the 1920s.

The automobile signaled the end of railroads as the main trans-
30   portation for people. It began an era of mobility in the United States that added greatly to its economic output. In the 1950s, the United States built a network of highways to link its vast territory. Today, there are well-maintained interstate highways that run from state to state. People can drive continuously
35   from coast to coast, or from Canada and Mexico, and to most locations in between. Today, most short-distance travel of people and goods is by road. Some long distance travel is also by road, but most long distance travel is by air and sea.

Automobiles consume over half the energy used for trans-
40   portation in the United States. They contribute heavily to the

(continued)

Practice Text 9-4 *(continued)*

---

nation's energy supply problems and to pollution. In some large cities major roads are packed with people during rush hour, the morning and evening hours when most people are going to and returning from work.

45 To help transport the great numbers of people, most large cities have some form of public transportation such as bus lines, subways, or commuter trains. People also ride together in car pools.

In an effort to find a solution to energy and environmental concerns, experimentation began with hybrid and electric pow-
50 ered automobiles. In 2000, the first hybrid automobiles became available to the public. These automobiles now get close to 50 miles per gallon of gas and emit much less pollution. Major auto manufacturers expect to be selling plug-in electric automobiles in the United States by 2010.

55 Here are some interesting facts about cars. One of the smallest cars ever built was only 4 feet and 4 inches long and had no reverse gear. One American limousine is equipped with a swimming pool and a helicopter landing pad. A flying car is now in production. It is designed to be used as a car and a plane.

60 Transportation has made significant progress since early civilization, With accommodation for the expanding population and for the fragile environment, the progress will continue.

I ask you to complete some comprehension questions after completing the second half of Exercise 9-4. Be sure to read for meaning as well as speed. Follow these steps to complete the second half of Exercise 9-4:

1. **Using a timer, read the essay again and strive to read to your new goal line.**

   This time, concentrate even harder. Did you make your goal of reading 25 percent more text? If not, try reading the essay a third time, and really focus this time to reach your goal.

2. **Answer the following comprehension questions.**

   I want you to answer these questions to make sure you don't sacrifice reading comprehension for reading speed. After all, the primary goal of reading is to comprehend, not to go fast. You should get at least four out of five answers right on the test. If you answer fewer than four questions correctly, you're putting too much emphasis on speed and not enough on comprehension. Focus more on your comprehension as you read.

Comprehension Questions

1. **In prehistoric times, the most common form of transportation was**

   A. On foot

   B. By horse

   C. By hot air balloon

   D. By bicycle

2. **Some scientists believe that wheeled vehicles first appeared in**

   A. Africa

   B. Canada

   C. South America

   D. The Middle East

3. **Modern transportation began in the late 1800s with the arrival of the**

   A. Electric train and street car

   B. Airplane and space travel

   C. Stagecoach and Pony Express

   D. Bicycle and steam engine

4. **Automobiles quickly became the chief means of passenger transportation in the 1920s because**

   A. Gas cost less than feeding and taking care of horses.

   B. Cars were mass produced on an assembly line and became more affordable.

   C. Cars were big enough to carry entire families.

   D. Cars didn't waste energy or cause air pollution.

5. **Today, most short-distance travel is by road and long-distance travel is by**

   A. Train

   B. Air and sea

   C. Car

   D. Private aircraft

Answer key: 1. A; **2.** D; **3.** A; **4.** B; **5.** C

Chapter 10

Other Reading Strategies to Supplement Your Speed Reading

• •

In This Chapter

▶ Skimming to get the gist

▶ Scanning for specific info

▶ Prereading to find out what to read

▶ Postreading for better retention

• •

This chapter takes a step away from speed reading and looks at other ways to gather information quickly from an article, book, or Web page. It describes skimming, scanning, prereading, and post-reading. You get tricks and techniques for doing these tasks and understand when to do them in lieu of speed reading.

Comparing Other Ways to Collect Info from Text

First, a little quiz. Which of the following is a speed-reading method?

A. Skimming

B. Scanning

C. Prereading

D. Speed reading

E. All of the above

F. None of the above

The correct answer is *E.* Skimming, scanning, and prereading, are strategies for supplementing your speed reading. They give you a solid notion of what you're reading and they help you locate the parts of the text that are worth reading. In the case of skimming and prereading, you familiarize yourself the text. When you return to the text and speed read it, that familiarity with the text increases your comprehension. Skimming and prereading are a bit like studying a map of an area you want to explore. You get the lay of the land so you can get more out of your explorations when you undertake them.

The following sections give you brief descriptions of skimming, scanning, and prereading. All the methods are described in more detail later in this chapter.

Skimming for the main ideas

When you skim a page, you take the main ideas from the reading material without reading all the words. You look for and seize upon words that appear to give the main meaning. If you're a newspaper reader, you already know what skimming is — you skim the headlines of the newspaper to decide which articles to read.

Readers skim when time is short or when they need to understand the general ideas but not the particulars of an article or book. Skimming occurs at three to four times the normal reading speed. For that reason, your reading comprehension takes a nose dive when you skim.

Skimming strategies include reading the first and last sentences of paragraphs, reading headings and subheadings, and studying tables and charts (and their captions). Later in this chapter, "Discovering the Art of Skimming" offers more detail on skimming strategies.

Studies show that people read and comprehend text on a computer screen more slowly than they read and comprehend printed material. Readers can't skim as efficiently on their computer screens either. When you read or skim a Web page on your computer, do so more slowly than usual if you want to read and skim efficiently.

Scanning for specific words or phrases

Scanning is quickly scouring the text for specific information; unlike skimming, you're not concerned with the broader meaning of the text. Scanning involves moving your eyes quickly down the page seeking specific words or phrases. It's the same technique you use when you look up a word in a telephone book or dictionary — you already know what you're looking for, and you concentrate on finding the word that provides the answer to your search.

Scan when you want to take one or two tidbits of information from a book or article. For example, to locate information about the California gold rush in an article about California history, you scan for the words *1849* or *gold rush.* After you find these words, you skim or carefully read only the part of the article where the words are located.

Obviously, your reading comprehension drops to just about nothing when you scan. Because you don't read for the author's ideas but try to pinpoint only what interests you, you lose the author's ideas. You don't comprehend anything except what happens to fall in your area of interest. Later in this chapter, "Scanning for the Information You Need" explains some scanning strategies.

Prereading to find out what the text is about

When you *preread,* you direct your attention to telltale parts of a text with the goal of finding out what the text is about, whether it's worth reading, and what parts to read. You typically use it in combination with another reading method; prereading just acts as the first filter. For example, to preread a company report, you read the headings, subheadings, table titles, and chart titles. Then you either dismiss the whole report because it isn't worth reading or you read the parts that are of interest to you.

Prereading is actually a technique for making better use of your reading time. Later in this chapter, "Prereading to Get the Lay of the Land" explains prereading in detail.

Discovering the Art of Skimming

Skimming is taking the most important information from the page without reading all the words. (The term comes from the act of skimming milk, when the dairy farmer skims the cream — the richest material — from the top of the milk before it's processed.) Strictly speaking, skimming isn't a reading technique but rather a scavenging technique. You hunt for the choicest information and hope important material doesn't pass you by.

You may already be a skimmer

Even speed readers skim a little bit. They gloss over connecting words and other little words in the course of their reading. In the interest of speed, words such as *the*, *and*, *for*, and *with* fall under the radar.

In this paragraph, I've removed the connecting and little words, but you can still get the meaning. This paragraph demonstrates what happens when you skim rather than read:

> Horse ran meadow to woods. We chased but soon lost sight where went. I called several times. Came back, looking tired, the harness still her neck.

This paragraph reads like an old-fashioned telegram, but you can understand the meaning. In the next paragraph, I restored the connecting and little words. Speed read it and note what happens when you come to a word I previously removed. You may well skip right over it.

> The horse ran through the meadow and to the woods. We chased after her but soon lost sight of where she went. I called out her name several times. Finally she came loping back, looking a little tired, with the harness still around her neck.

When you speed read, you skim to the extent that you don't fixate on all the words. In effect, you weed out some words and focus on the remaining ones. However, skimming takes the notion of passing by some words to another level. In the act of skimming, you focus only on the essential ideas and skip over the insignificant, marginal, and secondary. The question is, how can you recognize the essential ideas in the course of your skimming and focus on them, not the other ideas? The following sections help you get the most out of skimming.

Knowing when to skim

The first step in recognizing the essential ideas when you skim is knowing when to skim. Some materials and situations practically require skimming:

- ✔ Needlessly lengthy white papers and convoluted business reports are almost impossible not to skim.
- ✔ Newspapers, with their ready-made word clumps, are designed for skimming. (See Chapter 6 for more on reading in clumps.)
- ✔ If you're on a time crunch, you often have to skim because you don't have enough time to read the material.

But sometimes you can't find the essential ideas by skimming. If the reading material is especially meaty, you can't skim. You have to read or speed read the material. In much of your reading, you may even skim part of the article and read other parts. Think of skimming as an extra tool that you can use in addition to speed reading to get your reading done on time.

 Often a work's opening paragraphs and the concluding paragraphs present the author's main ideas. Opening paragraphs often outline what the author plans to prove, and closing paragraphs explain why the author's proof is justified. Read these paragraphs closely; don't skim them.

Bottom line: Use your judgment about when to skim. If you decide to skim, don't feel like you're losing something. You occasionally come across valuable material when you skim; when that happens, just stop skimming.

Grasping skimming techniques

Getting the essence from reading material without reading all the words boils down to knowing what parts to read and what parts to pass by. Following are some tips and techniques for recognizing what is important to read in the act of skimming.

Know what you want

Before you start skimming, ask yourself what you want to get from the book or article underneath your nose. Do you want to know about King Zog of Albania? Do you want to know how to sharpen an engraving tool? If you know exactly what you want from your reading, you can skim faster and better.

Think of two or three terms that describe what you want to know, and as you skim, keep an eye out for those two or three terms. Aimlessly skimming with no particular purpose can cause drowsiness, and eventually, sleep.

Read vertically as well as horizontally

When skimming, you move your eyes vertically as much as you move your eyes horizontally. In other words, you move your eyes down the page as much as you move them from side to side. Skimming is a bit like running down stairs. Yes, you should take one step at a time, and running down stairs is reckless, but you also get there faster by running.

Think like the author

Every chapter, article, book, and Web page is written to make an argument or point of some kind, and if you can detect the author's strategies for making his argument, you can separate the important from the unimportant material in the course of your reading. You can focus on the original, meaningful material and skip over the material that just supports the author's argument without advancing it.

Detecting the author's strategies requires you to put yourself in his place. Besides noticing the material on the page, notice *how* he presents the material. See whether you can recognize how the author places background material, secondary arguments, tangential information, and just plain frippery — anything that isn't essential to the thrust of his argument — that you can skip. Chapter 11 provides detailed information about how to think like an author.

For example, an article about oil production in Saudi Arabia may begin with two or three background pages about the history of oil development on the Arabian Peninsula. If you recognize these paragraphs as background (and you already know the history oil development in Saudi Arabia), you can skip them and save yourself a couple of pages.

Preread before you start skimming

As "Prereading to Get the Lay of the Land" explains later in this chapter, you preread to examine an article before you read it. By prereading an article before you skim, you can pinpoint the parts of the article that require your undivided attention and the parts that you can skip.

Try to detect the main idea in the introductory paragraphs

The introductory paragraphs usually express the main idea, argument, or goal of an article or chapter. Read these paragraphs closely. They tell you what the author's aim is, which can help you decide early on whether the article or chapter is worth reading in detail.

Sometimes the opening paragraphs, like a table of contents, lay out the course that the article or chapter takes. For example, scientific papers often begin by describing a problem of some kind, how the paper attempts to solve the problem, how others addressed the problem, and what conclusion the paper reaches.

Read the first sentence in each paragraph

The introductory sentence of each paragraph usually describes what follows in the paragraph. When you skim, read the first sentence in each paragraph and then decide whether the rest of the paragraph deserves a read. If it doesn't, move on.

Don't necessarily read complete sentences

When skimming, you don't even have to read complete sentences. If the start of a sentence holds no promise of the sentence giving you the information you want, skip to the next sentence. Read the start of sentences with an eye to whether they will yield useful information, and read them all the way through only if they appear to be useful at first glance.

Skip examples and proofs

Authors often present examples to prove a point, but if you believe the point doesn't need proving, you can skip the examples. For instance, suppose you're reading an article about the American Civil War in which the author says the war was inevitable. To prove the point, the article spends several pages looking into the slavery question, the differences between the economies of the North and South, and the polarizing 1860 presidential election. If you accept the author's premise that the war was inevitable, you can skim very quickly over the examples that prove this point because you don't need the proof.

Practicing skimming techniques

The two most important techniques to bear in mind when you skim are to move your eyes vertically as well as horizontally and to understand before you start skimming what information you're looking for. Exercise 10-1 is designed to give you a little practice skimming. Follow these steps to complete the exercise:

1. **Take a deep breath and brace yourself as though you're about to run the 100-meter dash.**

   Skimming requires as much concentration as you can muster. Get ready to go fast but also be thorough as you look for information on the page.

2. **Imagine that you're interested in getting the following information about the Internet: what was ARPANET, the predecessor of the Internet, and how does data travel on the Internet.**

3. **Start skimming "A Brief History of the Internet" by Peter Weverka (Practice Text 10-1), directing your eyes from black dot to black dot.**

   The black dots encourage you to read vertically as well as horizontally. Try to resist the urge to read horizontally only. Take in words with your peripheral vision.

Practice Text 10-1

A Brief History of the Internet

Most historians trace the beginning of the Internet to
Sputnik, the first satellite to successfully orbit the earth.
After Russia launched Sputnik in 1957, the United States
embarked on an ambitious national project to bridge what
was called the "technology gap" and catch up to the
Russians in science and technology. As part of that effort,
the Department of Defense established the Advanced
Research Projects Agency, or ARPA, in 1958. The Agency's
job was to oversee the research and development of new
technology for military use.

ARPA employed scientists and engineers in universities and
laboratories throughout the United States. These scientists
and engineers needed a way to exchange information and
collaborate with one another. To this end, ARPA developed
the first computer network, called ARPANET, in 1969. The
network permitted researchers throughout the United
States to dial in to and access four host computers — three
in California and one in Utah — over the telephone lines.

To speed the transmission of data, ARPANET employed a
novel means of sending information over the telephone
lines called packet switching. Instead of data being sent in a
continuous stream, it was divided into smaller units called
packets and sent all at once over available telephone lines.
Arriving at their destination, the packets were recompiled
— in other words, the data was reassembled so that it could
be read or interpreted. Like ARPANET, the Internet is a
packet-switching network. Packet switching makes it
possible for data to travel very quickly, because the packets
can arrive out of order, withstand delays in transmission,
and travel by many different routes to their destination. By
the strictest definition, the Internet is simply a
packet-delivery system. It can deliver information packets
anywhere in the world in less than a second.

ARPANET was the forerunner of the Internet. In ARPANET,
data did not pass through a central hub; instead, all the
host computers were connected to all the other host
computers. This revolutionary decentralized design
permitted data to take many different routes from one
computer to another because the computers were
interconnected. And if one part of the network failed, the
network's interconnectedness made it possible for other
parts to pick up the slack and continue transmitting data by

Practice Text 10-1 *(continued)*

---

a different route. Moreover, the decentralized structure of
ARPANET made it easier to add computers to the network.

In the beginning, only four host computers — computers
that other computers can connect to, similar to what we call
Web servers — were available on ARPANET, but universities
and research centers soon understood the value of being
able to collaborate over a network, and more host
computers were added. By 1971, there were 23 host
computers on ARPANET. In 1972, e-mail was invented so that
researchers could quickly exchange messages, and network
traffic increased dramatically. In 1977, ARPANET featured
111 host computers. By 1989, ARPANET had become a
"network of networks," with some 100,000 host computers,
and the Internet as you know it today had arrived.

Did you find out what ARPANET was? Did you discover how data
travels over the telephone lines on the Internet? This information
is in the essay. You really have to concentrate, and you have to
know what you're looking for, to skim successfully.

Scanning for the Information You Need

Think of scanning as a hyperactive form of skimming. You speed
through the text in search of information without any regard for the
overall gist of the author's ideas. All you want is information about
a specific topic — George Washington, the influenza virus, copper
production in 19th-century Peru, the Battle of Hastings, or whatever.
To help you become a top-notch scanner, the following sections give
you tips on scanning as well as a bit of scanning practice.

Getting the hang of scanning

When you're scanning, it helps to think in terms of targets. Think
of an informational target you want to hit and then try to hit it in
the text. Here are some other tips for scanning:

> ✔ **Use all your powers of concentration.** Scanning is boring as
> all get-out, so you may be inclined to slip into laziness. But if
> you get lazy and fail to concentrate, you won't find the infor-
> mation you want.

✔ **Scan for the two or three search terms that describe the information you want.** You can recognize terms more readily on the page if you have them in mind while you scan.

✔ **Use the Find command to scan a Web page.** Press Ctrl+F (the Find command), enter a search term, and press Enter. Your Web browser scrolls to the first instance of the search term you entered (if the term appears on the page at all).

✔ **Look at all italicized words.** According to popular publishing convention, authors often *italicize* and explain terms the first time they use them. If you're reading a printed book or magazine article that conforms to these conventional editorial standards, you can look to italicized words for explanations and perhaps for the information you need.

✔ **Don't be shy about using the table of contents and index.** Why scan when you can look up the information you need in the index? Why pore over numerous pages when the table of contents can direct you to the information you want?

Exercising your scanning skills

Exercise 10-2 demonstrates why scanning with a clear image of what you are looking for makes for more efficient scans. In the exercise, you look for the names of Alaskan cities in a large list:

1. **In Practice Text 10-2 scan for the name *Napakiak*.**

   Run your eyes down the list of names until you spy Napakiak.

2. **Go back to the beginning of the list and scan for the name *Bettles*.**

3. **Close your eyes for a moment and picture the letters in the name *Kasaan*.**

   This time, you'll have a picture in your mind when you scan.

4. **Start at the beginning of the list and scan for the name *Kasaan*.**

   Did you find it more quickly when you scanned with an image of the word?

5. **Close your eyes for a moment, picture the letters in the name *Egegik*, and then scan for it.**

   I hope this exercise demonstrated that scanning with a clear image of what you're looking for makes scans go faster.

Practice Text 10-2

Brevig Mission	Emmonak	Cold Bay	Kupreanof
North Pole	Sand Point	Kaktovik	Pilot Point
Saxman	Shaktoolik	Sitka	Fort Yukon
Chefornak	Teller	Egegik	Newhalen
St. Michael	Shageluk	Chuathbaluk	Anvik
Old Harbor	Allakaket	Nightmute	Buckland
Shungnak	Soldotna	Circle Hot Springs	Circle
Chignik	Shishmaref	Angoon	Coffman Cove
Juneau	Kwethluk	Alakanuk	Ekwok
Kake	Palmer	Chevak	Ketchikan
Napaskiak	New Stuyahok	Grayling	St. Mary's
Thorne Bay	Wrangell	Ouzinkie	Fairbanks
Russian Mission	Pelican	Kotzebue	Atka
Bethel	White Mountain	Eek	Anderson
Upper Kalskag	Kaltag	Napakiak	Cordova
Ambler	Akhiok	Klawock	Unalaska
Unalakleet	Akiak	Quinhagak	Nome
Koyukuk	Goodnews Bay	Kasaan	Akutan
Toksook Bay	Kachemak	Tok	Nunapitchuk
Whittier	Tanana	Gustavus	Bettles
Savoonga	Kenai	Kodiak	Gambell
Selawik	Kobuk	Larsen Bay	Kivalina
Aleknagik	Anchorage	St. George	Eagle
Nulato	Central	Scammon Bay	Anaktuvuk Pass
King Cove	False Pass	Seldovia	Deering
Port Alexander	Golovin	Port Heiden	Lower Kalskag
Nondalton	Clark's Point	Adak	Togiak
Nikolai	Atqasuk	Nenana	Koyuk
Nunam Iqua	Craig	Yakutat	Wasilla
Nuiqsut	Kotlik	Noorvik	Dillingham

Prereading to Get the Lay of the Land

Prereading is a bit like sizing up an item before you buy it. You wouldn't buy the brand-new car without driving it around the block first, so why should you spend a bunch of time reading a book or article without sizing it up beforehand? Prereading can be a real timesaver.

Prereading involves examining the main features of a book, magazine article, or Web page before you read it to find out whether it or parts of it are worth reading. In the following sections, I show you where to find these features and how to judge the value of reading material by prereading it.

Sizing up the reading material

No matter what type of reading material you're faced with, you can tell a lot about it by prereading these important features:

- ✔ **Title:** You can't judge a book by its cover, but you can often judge it by its title. With luck, the title is descriptive and includes, as so many titles do, an equally descriptive subtitle to help you decide whether this is the book or article you're looking for.

- ✔ **Author:** Look at the author's credentials to find out whether the author knows the topic. If you had to choose between two articles about molecular biology, and the author of one article was a biologist and the other a theologian, which article would you choose?

- ✔ **Publication date:** Take note of the publication date to see whether the book or article is up-to-date (if that matters in your reading). Look for a book's publication date on the back of the title page.

- ✔ **Headings and subheadings:** Examine headings to find out what information is in the book. They also give you a sense of how well the author organizes information and builds to a conclusion. If the headings and subheadings describe topics that are all over the map and don't logically follow one another, you may be looking at a book or article that isn't well thought out — or worth reading.

✔ **Graphics, charts, and tables:** Study these visuals and any accompanying captions; they provide a vivid picture of the information offered in the article or book and can give you a clue as to whether you'll find the info you're looking for.

✔ **Paragraph length:** Thumb through the book or article to get a sense of how many paragraphs it has and the average paragraph length. Each paragraph typically presents a single thought. Generally speaking, therefore, an article with many short paragraphs presents many thoughts but doesn't elaborate on them; an article with many long paragraphs doesn't present as many thoughts but is more thorough in describing each one.

After you finish prereading, estimate how much time you need to speed read the article, chapter, or Web page. Chapter 5 explains how to calculate your words-per-minute reading speed. If you know your reading speed and roughly how many words are in the reading material, you can estimate your reading time by dividing the total number of words by your words-per-minute rate.

Getting some prereading practice

Exercise 10-3 is designed to give you a little prereading practice and help you understand what to examine in a chapter or article you preread. The exercise presents two versions of the same essay: one that highlights the material you preread and fills in the rest of the essay with nonsense, and a second that gives you the entire essay. You preread in the first essay and then read the entire second essay, answering a set of questions after each reading to compare how much you pick up by prereading with how much you gather by reading. You may discover that sometimes prereading is almost as fruitful as regular reading.

Follow these steps to complete the first half of Exercise 10-3:

1. **Preread the first version of the essay "Commit to Making Positive Changes" (Practice Text 10-3a).**

   I've boldfaced the material you want to focus your prereading on and turned the other text into Latin nonsense. Pay attention to the bolded information because that's what the end-of-reading-quiz covers.

2. **Take the prereadng questions quiz.**

   Note your score so you can compare it to your second quiz score later in the exercise.

Practice Text 10-3a

Commit to Making Positive Changes
by Tom Hopkins

In my seminars and my books, I have a lot to say about the vast importance of having goals voluptate, felis nec nulla, urna wisi amet dignissim suspendisse.

I'm not alone in believing that goals are vital; sodales aliquam arcu ut lobortis ligula, amet integer elit tempora maecenas ut. Nulla pharetra nibh pellentesque.

Ligula, amet **review the basic rules of putting the power of goals to work for you.**

- **Write your goals down**. Ut per, aliquam non duis aenean, nec nullam interdum sit curabitur duis, dui tempor dui id justo nibh pellentesque.

- **Review your goals regularly**. Nec nulla, urna wisi amet dignissim suspendisse vestibulum.

- **Keep your goals with you.** Dolor nam, velit quis quam in amet diam. Malesuada turpis sodales dolor voluptate, felis nec nulla, urna wisi amet dignissim suspendisse vestibulum, nam vestibulum vitae aliquam laoreet est mattis pellentesque.

- **Make sure your goals are realistic**. Dictum ut sodales litora justo penatibus, earum urna, eros ac, volutpat amet, felis nec nulla, urna wisi amet dignissim non duis aenean in magna eros sem in ipsum.

Nulla pharetra nibh **the second goal I wrote down as a long-term goal when I was 21 years old.** Eu curabitur, turpis adipiscing nascetur vivamus.

I was sitting in an airplane. It was my first flight. Nulla pharetra nibh pellentesque consectetuer arcu, nulla euismod, euismod ridiculus malesuada dolor nam, velit quis quam in amet diam. Malesuada turpis sodales dolor voluptate, felis nec nulla, urna wisi amet dignissim suspendisse magna eros sem in ipsum suspendisse.

I asked the man next to me, "What is that cute little plane?" Lorem ipsum dolor sit amet, integer condimentum lacus ultricies egestas posuere sodales, turpis praesentium imperdiet nulla tellus vehicula.

Now the surprising thing about a goal that's in writing is, if you concentrate on it every day, it will become real. Commodo phasellus ut per, aliquam non duis aenean, nec nullam interdum sit curabitur duis, dui tempor dui id justo. Dictum ut sodales

---

Practice Text 10-3a *(continued)*

---

litora justo penatibus, earum urna, eros ac, volutpat amet. Nulla pharetra nibh pellentesque consectetuer arcu, nulla euismod, ut sodales euismod.

Elit vitae etiam laoreet morbi, quis torquent ac a ipsum. Eu curabitur, turpis adipiscing.

I'll never forget the first time we landed to refuel. Nam egestas mauris eleifend ac sed condimentum, et eleifend, ipsum tempus, ipsum felis pede nullam vivamus viverra integer velit.

That long-term goal turned out to be a $30,000-per-month goal, which turned out to be unrealistic for me. Fusce scelerisque malesuada sollicitudin mi, blandit ipsum nullam porttitor eget quod pellentesque, dignissim fringilla nunc sed maecenas, nec pulvinar rutrum augue proin, eu donec elit molestie dolor non.

Eu curabitur, **one thing you have to realize about long-term goals is there will be times when you've got to make decisions to change your goals**. Volutpat et nulla est tempor, id donec lectus sit, leo sit cursus conubia placerat eget hymenaeos et nulla.

- **Act on your goals.** Felis pede nullam vivamus, non wisi mattis.

- **Give yourself rewards for achieving a goal**. Dignissim fringilla nunc sed maecenas, nec pulvinar rutrum augue proin, eu donec elit molestie dolor non.

- **Plan how you'll make your goals happen**. Nam egestas mauris eleifend ac sed condimentum, et eleifend, ipsum tempus, ipsum felis pede.

- **Resolve conflicts between goals immediately.** Nam egestas mauris eleifend ac sed condimentum, et eleifend, ipsum tempus, ipsum felis pede nullam vivamus, est pellentesque consectetuer non wisi mattis. Id donec arcu tristique vel mauris, dui faucibus praesent ullamcorper quam quis.

- **Make your goals relevant to your family.** Curabitur netus eros aliquam, nullam pretium, pellentesque nec mauris tempus, odio ipsum elit, curabitur sed eget adipiscing massa tortor. Faucibus tincidunt, in risus, gravida etiam nisl, maecenas ante orci, quisque luctus pharetra orci. Fusce scelerisque malesuada sollicitudin mi, blandit ipsum nullam porttitor.

(continued)

Practice Text 10-3a *(continued)*

- **Preserve the inspiration of your goals by keeping them up to date.** In metus at. Eu malesuada nulla, quisque sapien, condimentum id arcu. Sit pretium tincidunt diam a nulla rerum. Volutpat nullam pretium, pellentesque nec mauris tempus, odio ipsum elit.

- **Recap your goals annually**. Fusce scelerisque malesuada sollicitudin mi, blandit ipsum nullam porttitor eget quod pellentesque, dignissim fringilla nunc sed maecenas, nec pulvinar rutrum augue proin, eu donec elit molestie dolor non.

Prereading Questions

1. **Does Tom Hopkins support the importance of having goals?**

   A. Yes — he discusses it in his books and seminars.

   B. He personally feels goal-setting is important.

   C. He joins other experts in supporting goal-setting.

   D. All of the above.

2. **Does Hopkins have rules for putting goals to work for you?**

   A. No, he doesn't think rules are important.

   B. Yes, he thinks goal-setting rules are very important.

   C. Keep changing rules to set new goals.

   D. Keep reviewing rules.

3. **What was Hopkins's first goal?**

   A. The reading selection doesn't say.

   B. He forgot to define his first goal.

   C. His first goal was a big mistake.

   D. His first goal was to become rich and successful.

4. **Does Hopkins discuss his other goals?**

   A. He lists his first five goals.

   B. He discusses the importance of each goal.

   C. He only discusses the second goal he ever set.

   D. He discusses how he set his third goal.

5. **Which of these is/are Hopkins's rule(s) for benefitting from your long term goals?**

   A. Act on your goals.

   B. Make your goals family-relevant.

   C. Change them as necessary.

   D. All of the above.

   Answer key: 1: D; **2:** B; **3:** A; **4:** C; **5:** D

To complete the second half of Exercise 10-3,

1. **Speed read the second version of "Commit to Making Positive Changes" (Practice Text 10-3b).**

   This time, you can read the entire essay.

2. **Take the speed-reading questions quiz and note your score in Appendix B.**

Practice Text 10-3b

Commit to Making Positive Changes
by Tom Hopkins, author of *Selling For Dummies*, 2nd Edition
Originally published in 1980

In my seminars and my books, I have a lot to say about the vast importance of having goals that pull you forward, instead of relying on your ordinary needs to drive you.

I'm not alone in believing that goals are vital; practically every modern thinker or speaker on the subject of success extols the benefits of goal setting.

So let's review the basic rules of putting the power of goals to work for you.

- Write your goals down. Unwritten goals are wishes that do nothing; written goals are active contracts you've made with yourself.

- Review your goals regularly. Otherwise they'll fade from your memory and amount to zero.

- Keep your goals with you. If you keep the cards you've written your goals on with you, you can review and revise them in spare moments. The whole idea is to make them a living, vital part of your life and a powerful influence on your daily decisions.

(continued)

Practice Text 10-3b *(continued)*

- Make sure your goals are realistic. Goals you don't believe you can achieve are worse than useless because they blind you to goals you could achieve. And, they discourage your belief in the whole goal-setting and achieving process.

Let me tell you about the second goal I wrote down as a long-term goal when I was 21 years old. This is how vivid I want goal setting to become.

I was sitting in an airplane. It was my first flight. I was flying from California to Arizona. I'd never been in a plane before. You might remember your first flight. I was sitting there scared to death. We were taking off, and I looked out the window to the right and on the runway next to our plane, this beautiful little plane took off.

I asked the man next to me, "What is that cute little plane?" He said, "That's a jet — a corporate jet." I said, "Boy, that's cute." I took out my goal setting device right then and there and wrote it down — "jet, ten-year goal."

Now the surprising thing about a goal that's in writing is, if you concentrate on it every day, it will become real. I will never forget the day that the jet arrived. It was ten years later to the day. I had just finished a program in Baton Rouge, LA, and as I stood there on that runway and that little plane came out, I thought, "This is it. Ten years and I've arrived."

When I got on the plane, the pilot welcomed me on. I said, "This is it. I've arrived."

And do you know what happened? After awhile, it's just another thing. A fun toy. A big toy.

I'll never forget the first time we landed to refuel. The pilot came back and said, "We've refueled," and handed the receipt to me — $882. I said, "Is this for the month?" It wasn't.

That long-term goal turned out to be a $30,000-per-month goal; which turned out to be unrealistic for me. Even though I was earning enough to afford it, I always thought of it as an extravagance. It was out of my comfort zone for me to have that plane. It just wasn't a part of my reality. That's why I only had it for two months.

You see, one thing you have to realize about long-term goals is there will be times when you've got to make decisions to change your goals. Some people are so afraid of a long-term goal, though, they'll set no goals. That's the sad part of it.

Practice Text 10-3b *(continued)*

- Act on your goals. Nothing happens unless you make it happen.

- Give yourself rewards for achieving a goal. Your drive to achieve will wither and die if you don't feed it some benefits at least once in a while.

- Plan how you'll make your goals happen. If you don't plan in detail how your goals will be achieved, how can you make them happen?

- Resolve conflicts between goals immediately. People often set up goals that are in direct conflict with each other: Spend more time with the kids; spend more time planning and preparing for sales work. When you discover such a conflict, it alerts you to the necessity of making hard choices and scheduling more effectively.

- Make your goals relevant to your family. Unless you involve your family in them, your goals will conflict with the aims of your loved ones. This is certain to increase tension within your family and make the achievement of your purposes more difficult. Don't leave them out; instead, get them on your side. "If I win this sales contest, we'll all go to Disneyland."

- Preserve the inspiration of your goals by keeping them up to date. Your life is dynamic; your desires and capabilities are under constant change. New information may at any time make some or all of your present goals obsolete. When things change for you, change your goals. They're not carved on Mount Rushmore.

- Recap your goals annually. At the end of the year, go over every goal you've set the previous year and see how much you've really accomplished. This is a great motivator in which to launch a whole new, even more productive year.

Comprehension Questions

1. **Why does Tom Hopkins value goal-setting so highly?**

    A. Because setting goals provides special incentive to move you forward

    B. Because normal motivations are insufficient

    C. Because all experts agree that goal setting is critical for success

    D. Because you need a sense of humor

2. **How many are the basic rules for triggering the power of goals?**

    A. Only one

    B. Two: writing down the goals and reviewing them

    C. Four

    D. You set your own number of basic rules to follow.

3. **What incident made Hopkins rethink a goal he had set?**

    A. He realized he didn't want to travel so much.

    B. During a trip, he realized the goal he'd set wasn't realistic for him.

    C. He discovered the cost of fuel for his private plane.

    D. He made a decision to slow down in his work.

4. **According to Hopkins, why are goals put down in writing more powerful?**

    A. Your concentration is focused.

    B. You feel obligated to make the goal come true.

    C. Experience of experts demonstrates that that's the way to reach your goals.

    D. You don't want to forget them.

5. **When does Hopkins say you change goals?**

    A. When common sense dictates

    B. When family situation changes

    C. When alternative goals need consideration

    D. All of the above

Answer key: 1: A; **2:** C; **3:** B; **4:** C; **5:** D

How did your score on the two quizzes compare? I'm betting you scored equally well on both quizzes. I also hope that this exercise demonstrated how valuable prereading is. Sometimes you can get away with prereading an article or chapter without reading it because prereading points you to the parts of reading material that you really need to focus on.

Postreading to Reinforce What You Read

After you finish reading an article, chapter, or Web page, consider *postreading* it, or rereading the essential parts. In a postread, you know where the essential parts are and you can find and read them very quickly.

Postreading is an excellent way to retain what you have read. It locks the information you acquired into your long-term memory. Postread all material you'll be tested on or material that is important to your job or career — in short, postread whatever you want to lock away in your memory. (Head to Chapter 3 for more info on short- and long-term memory.)

Here's a great way to retain what you read: Describe it to yourself. After you finish reading an article, for example, summarize it. Outline the key points and describe the conclusion as though you wrote the article yourself. Putting an article in your own words makes it easier to remember. Studies show that on average you forget 40 to 50 percent of what you read unless you make a conscious effort to remember it.

Chapter 11

Taking Advantage of Writing Structure to Read More Quickly

- -

In This Chapter

▶ Getting the gist of a paragraph

▶ Following the author's thought patterns

▶ Taking your cue from signal words

▶ Skipping subordinate clauses

- -

*W*hat if you could wave a magic wand over a book or article and instantly see only the information you need? You'd save hours of labor separating the information you need from the information you don't need.

Scientists are still many years away from perfecting this magic wand. Until they perfect it, this chapter provides tips and tricks to help you locate the information you want and bypass needless information without a magic wand. This chapter further refines the reading strategies in Chapter 10 by showing you where to look in a paragraph to detect the main thrust or idea. It suggests how you can follow the author's line of thought throughout an essay and in so doing take from the essay only the information that's useful to you. It also explains how signal words can guide you to information and how you can save time by skirting subordinate clauses.

The techniques described in this chapter are especially useful when taking standardized tests. In these tests, when time is of the essence, being able to quickly pick up the author's meaning, and knowing when you can skim or skip ahead, is vital. Head to Chapter 13 for more on speed reading standardized tests.

Getting to the Main Idea in a Paragraph with Topic Sentences

You may remember from your English composition class that all writing is constructed from paragraphs and that each paragraph is supposed to present one idea. A complex idea requires a long paragraph consisting of many sentences, whereas a simple idea requires only a sentence or two. Strung together, the paragraphs present an argument or narrative of some kind. For example, they describe a trip across the wilds of Borneo or the behavior of the stock market in the past five decades.

Going straight to the main idea of each paragraph significantly increases your reading speed. You don't have to read as much to get a firmer grasp of the author's fundamental ideas. (This quality differentiates it from *skimming*, a reading method in which you look at headings, captions, and so on to quickly find a work's overall meaning. See Chapter 10 for more on skimming.)

The question is: How do you recognize the main idea in a paragraph amid all the details? How do you zoom to what really matters in each paragraph?

Understanding topic sentences

The best way to get the main idea in a paragraph is to locate the *topic sentence.* This sentence describes the subject of the paragraph and its main idea. If you can develop a nose for locating topic sentences, you can get the main idea from paragraphs quickly and thereby improve your reading speed.

Typically, the topic sentence comes first in a paragraph, and the remaining sentences elaborate on the topic sentence. In this paragraph, for example, the topic sentence makes a simple assertion, and evidence for the truth of this assertion follows on the heels of the topic sentence:

> Rainfall has been increasing steadily in Yoknapatawpha County since 1995. In that year, annual rainfall was 32 inches. By 2008, it was 40 inches, with an increase each year between 1995 and 2008, except for 1999, when the annual rainfall level fell to 29 inches.

But sometimes the topic sentence isn't the first sentence in the paragraph. Sometimes it's buried deeper. In this paragraph, the second sentence is the topic sentence:

> Looking at rainfall in Yoknapatawpha County since 1995, a clear trend is evident. Except for 1999, when the annual rainfall level fell to 29 inches, rainfall has increased steadily since 1995. Between that year and 2008, rainfall rose from 32 to 40 inches annually.

The author of the following paragraph is a bit of a windbag and takes his time getting to the main idea. In this paragraph, the topic sentence is the last sentence:

> Is it getting wetter or drier in Yoknapatawpha County? A quick look at the record gives a clear answer. Between 1995 and 2008, rainfall rose from 32 to 40 inches annually (although in 1999 it dipped to 29 inches). From this information, it's plain to see that rainfall in the county has increased steadily since 1995.

Locating the topic sentence

Because the topic sentence can be located anywhere, how can you spot the topic sentence and get to the main idea in a paragraph? Here's how:

- ✓ **Read the first sentence carefully.** Three times out of five, the topic sentence is the first sentence.

- ✓ **Consider what basic property or characteristic of the paragraph describes.** This attribute is the paragraph's main idea, so the sentence that expresses it is your topic sentence.

- ✓ **Think about the paragraph's purpose.** The paragraph most likely wants to impart a particular piece of information. If you can figure out what that piece is, you know the paragraph's topic and can find the sentence that presents it.

 Observe the author's writing style to determine where she likes to put the topic sentence in paragraphs. After you've spent some time with an author, you can begin to see where he or she likes to put topic sentences. In formal writing, the topic sentence almost always comes first in paragraphs. Chatty writers tend to put the topic sentence in the middle or end of paragraphs. Knowing your author's style helps you locate the topic sentence faster.

Thinking Like the Author

Different authors use different strategies in their work, and if you can identify and detect these strategies, you can find and absorb the author's ideas more efficiently. This section explains how to do just that by taking knowledge levels into account and paying attention to structure.

A good way to detect the author's strategy for presenting ideas is to turn quickly through the text, paying special attention to headings.

Taking knowledge level into account

Every book and article assumes that the reader has a certain amount of knowledge of the topic at hand. For example, I wrote the *For Dummies* book you're currently reading on the assumption that you're a beginning speed reader. If I were writing this book for an audience of reading educators, I would assume they already have a background in speed-reading techniques, and I wouldn't spend as much time describing speed-reading fundamentals.

Consider yourself lucky if every article and book you read is written to your knowledge level. Usually you have to read above your knowledge level or below it because the material is more complex than you want or too simple for your needs.

After you've had a taste of the article or book you're reading, consider what knowledge level it's written to and change your reading accordingly:

- ✔ If the reading material is too complex for your taste, read a little more slowly. You're likely to encounter terminology and background information that you don't know.

- ✔ If the reading material is simpler than what you need, read quickly and skim where you can. Read more aggressively than usual and cherry-pick information from the text.

Paying attention to structure

Essays and articles, like buildings, must have a structure or framework if they're going to hold up, and you can make your reading more efficient if you pay attention to structure. After you know how a piece is structured, you can focus on the parts that interest you and skim or skip the rest. The following sections describe some common writing structures.

The basic essay

In its most basic form, an essay has the following structure (you may remember this from school):

1. Introduction describing what's in the essay and what the essay aims to prove or demonstrate

2. Argument presenting facts in order of significance supporting the essay's argument

3. Conclusion summarizing the facts with a statement declaring how the facts support the argument

To quickly read this kind of essay, you can read the introduction to see whether the essay is worth reading, read the facts that are unknown to you (skipping the known facts), and read the conclusion only if you need more convincing or you're unsure how the argument leads to the conclusion. In a basic essay, the conclusion is foreshadowed by the introduction, so reading the conclusion is optional.

The news story

News stories like the kind found in newspapers also have a simple structure because they're written to be read quickly. In the opening paragraph, the author tells you the when, where, what, why, who, and how. After that, the story presents ever-widening levels of detail with the idea that you can quit reading whenever you want. News stories don't end with summary conclusions. The structure of a news story looks something like this:

1. Introduction explaining when, where, what, and how

2. Body presenting increasingly more refined details and background information

Compare and contrast

The *compare-and-contrast structure* presents items, ideas, and so on to describe a topic and highlight its special qualities. For example, an author may compare the public transportation systems of Paris and Tokyo to highlight challenges facing civil engineers.

In this structure, the author introduces several subtopics one at a time and then draws comparisons and makes contrasts. While you read, take note when a new subtopic begins and skip or skim it if you're already familiar with it. Slow down for subtopics with information that's new to you.

Division and subdivision

The *division-and-subdivision structure* divides a topic into subtopics and further subtopics to make it easier to understand. This kind of piece can be the easiest or most difficult to read, depending on whether the author wrote descriptive headings and subheadings:

- ✔ If the author writes a good heading, you can preread the headings and subheadings to locate the information you need. (Chapter 10 explains prereading.)

- ✔ If the headings aren't descriptive, skim the essay to get a sense of how it's divided into topics and subtopics and try to locate the information that's meaningful to you.

Cause and effect

Authors use the *cause-and-effect structure* to explain why an event or condition (such as lung cancer) occurs and what its consequences are.

The cause-and-effect structure looks something like this:

1. Causes of the event

2. The event

3. Consequences of the event

As a reader of a cause-and-effect essay, you can save time by distinguishing between the direct and indirect causes (if the author doesn't do a good job of it), and focus on the direct causes. You can also save time by focusing on the area (causes, event, or consequences) with the information you need.

Chronological

In the *chronological structure,* the author describes events according to a timeline, with the earliest event first and the others following after. History articles are almost always written this way.

 As you read a chronological essay, always remember what year or time period you're reading about and note how one subject links to the next. Doing so helps you retain what you read.

Looking Out for Signal Words

Signal words tell you where the author is going next, and if you're alert to these words, you can improve your reading efficiency. You can tell what direction the author is going in and judge right away whether to keep reading, skim, or skip ahead. Signal words cue you to the author's line of thought. They tell you when the author is about to present a contrast, comparison, conclusion, additional argument, or example. Keeping an eye out for signal words can make you a more efficient reader because signal words help you decide whether to keep reading, skim, or skip ahead.

Contrast signals

Contrast signals introduce a thought or description that contrasts with a previously described thought or description. Contrast signals include

> although, but, conversely, despite, however, instead, in opposition, on the contrary, on the other hand, nevertheless, nonetheless, rather than, still, then again, while

Here are examples of how contrast signals are used:

> The team lost many of its important players to injury. Nevertheless, the team remained a formidable opponent.

> Although Munich was the most populous city in West Germany, Bonn, a small university town, was the capital.

> Rather than study fungi as they did until quite recently, mycologists now study yeasts.

When you encounter a contrast signal and believe that the author is about to draw a contrast, decide whether reading the contrasting thought will clarify the author's argument. If you don't need a clarification, skim or skip ahead.

Comparison signals

Comparison signals tell you when the author is going to compare what was already described to something new. Comparisons underscore the similarities and differences between objects, concepts, and so on to bring these characteristics to light. Comparison signals include

> and, by comparison, by the same token, correspondingly, equally, in the same way, likewise, similarly

These examples demonstrate how comparison signals are used:

> By comparison to the Greeks, the Romans were also excellent scientists, especially in the field of engineering.

> Similarly, Placido Domingo had a strong tenor voice and a keen acting ability.

> Likewise, the next governor faced many economic problems, and he had few resources for tackling them.

If you understand the quality being described that the author wants to illuminate with a comparison, don't bother reading the comparison. Skim or skip ahead.

Example signals

Example signals are pretty self-explanatory: They introduce an example. After all, using an example is the easiest and best way to strengthen an argument. Here are some common example signals:

> as an example, for example, for instance

Here are some sample example signals (say *that* five times fast):

> Construction costs have risen precipitously. As an example, the cost of sheetrock has risen from 1 to 2 dollars per square foot.

> Forest eco-systems are susceptible to a variety of disturbances. For example, fires typically occur at a 30- to 50-year interval.

> All is not well in Denmark. For instance, consider last year's presidential election.

If you're in agreement with the author and don't require an example to understand his point, skim or skip over the example.

Additional argument signals

Additional argument signals cue you when the author is about to give more reasons to support her argument. These signals include

> also, and, as well, besides, furthermore, in addition, moreover, what's more

Check out these examples of additional argument signals:

> The ancients considered it a remedy for the common cold. They also took it for breathing ailments and allergies.

> Besides, the knights carried another weapon to strike terror in their opponents — the longbow.

> You can visit the outstanding art museums and galleries. Moreover, you can spend the day at one of the city's many beaches.

If you're already convinced by the author's argument, you can skim or skip ahead when you come to an additional argument signal. Keep reading if you remain unconvinced and you still want to be persuaded.

Causation signals

Causation signals tell you that the author is about to describe the result of a previously described activity or phenomenon. Causation signals include

> as, because, consequently, given that, for this reason, owing to, seeing that, since, therefore, thus

Here are some causation signals in action:

> It was much too cold even for ice fishing. Therefore, they stayed home and watched hockey on TV.

> Owing to a lack of foresight and planning, they had to declare bankruptcy.

> Because of this simple oversight, the wall crumbled and the plain was flooded.

When you encounter a causation signal, decide whether you already know the result (or it's worth knowing). Then skim or skip ahead if you don't need or care to know the result.

Conclusion signals

Conclusion signals indicate when the author is about to draw a conclusion. Typically, conclusion signals appear at the bottom of a paragraph or article. Conclusion signals include

> accordingly, as a result, consequently, finally, in brief, in conclusion, in short, in sum

These examples show how authors use conclusion signals:

> Finally, when the verdict was delivered, it became a matter not for us but for the law books.

> In conclusion, there are only three types of soil according to this parable — where the ground is hard, where it is rocky, and where it is capable of sprouting seeds.

> The audience accordingly left the theater in a state of bewilderment, wondering what they had just witnessed.

When you see a conclusion signal, keep reading if a wrap-up of what you just read is useful to you; if the conclusion is foregone in your opinion, skim or skip ahead.

Recognizing and Skipping Subordinate Clauses

Subordinate clauses get that name for a reason: They convey information that is secondary to the essential idea or thrust of the sentence. Subordinate clauses are sometimes called *dependent clauses* because they depend on other parts of the sentence to give them meaning.

In the following example sentence, the subordinate clause tells you how long the country waited, but this information is secondary to the real news — that the king was safe (I put the subordinate clause in italics so that you can find it more easily):

> The entire country, *which had been waiting for weeks for news about the king,* learned that he was safe in the castle.

Because subordinate clauses convey secondary information, consider skimming or skipping them when you're in a hurry. The easiest way to recognize a subordinate clause is to look for the relative pronouns that typically introduce subordinate clauses:

> which, whichever, who, whoever, whom, whose, whomever, whosoever

Exercise 11-1 gives you practice in recognizing subordinate clauses and demonstrates why skipping these clauses can save you time. In the exercise, you read two sets of sentences. In the first set, you read the entire sentence, and in the second, you skip over the subordinate clauses. Afterward, you note how long it took to read each set of sentences.

Follow these steps to complete the first half of Exercise 11-1:

1. **Using a timer, read Sentences 1 through 10 of Practice Text 11-1 in their entirety and note where the subordinate clauses occur.**

   Each sentence contains one subordinate clause.

2. **In Appendix B, mark down how long you take to read Sentences 1 through 10.**

Practice Text 11-1

---

1. The Sierra Madre, which is the tallest of the mountain ranges, loomed in the distance.

2. We worried because Mr. Haines, who owned the dog, had recently left the city.

3. The people whose cheers egged him on were suddenly ashamed.

4. The woman, who wore a gray blouse and skirt, left her keys there.

5. Whichever makes the grade, St. Louis or Detroit, will win the prize.

6. The carpenter, who does very fine work, is available now.

7. Whoever they turn out to be, the outlaw gang will be punished accordingly.

8. Poor old Bill, whose car it was, thanked the firefighters.

9. Ms. Watson, who supervised the construction of the building, said it was complete.

10. The apple pie, which turned out to be delicious, was sitting on the window sill.

Follow these steps to complete the second half of Exercise 11-1:

1. **Again using a timer, read sentences 11 through 20, skipping the subordinate clauses.**

   When you see the relative pronouns *which, who,* or *whose,* skip ahead.

2. **Note how long you take to read Sentences 11 through 20 in Appendix B.**

Practice Text 11-1 *(continued)*
---

11. A single church spire, which came to a narrow point, stood out against the sky.

12. We shouted at the cat, which kept scratching us, to cut it out.

13. The baseball players whose bats they were told us to stay and watch the game.

14. The man, who wore a stripped shirt and short pants, ran away.

15. Whichever comes first. the Chevy or the Ford, will receive our praise

16. The student, who is first in her class, is waiting for us.

17. Whoever they are, the whole kit and caboodle are in for a surprise.

18. Ms. Wilcox, whose house we visited, knew him too.

19. The dean, who was forced to apologize, looked upset.

20. The trophy case, which turned out to be made of glass, shined in the brilliant light.

I'm betting you took less time to read the second set of sentences. I'm also guessing that you lost very little in terms of comprehension when you skipped over the subordinate clauses. When you're in a hurry, glide over subordinate clauses without reading them or paying them much attention.

Part IV

Improving Your Comprehension

The 5th Wave   By Rich Tennant

SPEED READING MOMS

"Well, I can't say Kyle's essays have improved, but it's nice that I can now reach their disappointing conclusion in 8.7 seconds."

In this part...

What's the use of reading if you don't understand the author's words? Part IV looks into the all-important matter of how to improve your comprehension when you read.

Take a look at Chapter 12 for guidance on improving your vocabulary. Chapter 13 is a catchall chapter with information on speed reading while taking standardized tests and reading textbooks and newspapers, among other things. Regardless of your situation, you're sure to find something useful in Chapter 13.

Chapter 12

Expanding Your Vocabulary to Become a Better Speed Reader

*T*he larger your vocabulary is, the faster you can read because you don't stumble as often on words you don't know or recognize. When you read words that you're already familiar with, you read beyond the words for their meanings. In the act of reading, you absorb ideas, thoughts, feelings, and descriptions, not individual words. You see the forest, not the trees.

This chapter offers advice for expanding your vocabulary so you can become a better speed reader. It explains how you acquire new vocabulary words and how you recognize and interpret prefixes, root words, and suffixes in words.

 By the way, be sure to check out Appendix A if you are interested in expanding your vocabulary. Appendix A lists *prime words,* the 2,000 most common words in the English language. Prime words comprise about 75 percent of words you encounter in your reading, so mastering them goes a long way toward knowing the words you need in your reading.

Understanding How Your Vocabulary Expands

Educators debate about how to enlarge children's vocabularies. One side says to have them memorize words, and the other is in favor of giving them more reading experience and trusting them to grasp new vocabulary words in reading material that is meaningful to them. I side with the second group.

When most people hear the word *vocabulary,* they have dreary memories of the former kind of vocabulary instruction. Typically, the teacher would give out a list of vocabulary words, and you'd look up the words in a dictionary and write down their definitions. A day or so later, you took a quiz on the words, and you had to regurgitate their definitions on a piece of ruled paper (which made you kind of nauseated for real). You wondered whether you'd ever have the occasion to use the vocabulary words in real life.

Unfortunately for schoolchildren the world over, memorizing vocabulary words is one of the least efficient ways to expand your vocabulary. Studies show that you learn new words best when the words have meaning for you or you discover them in context.

Discovering vocabulary words by meaning

No matter how arcane or hard to pronounce it is, you can pick up and retain a new word if it has meaning for you. Studies show that the best way to acquire more vocabulary words is by real-world experience, not artificial memorization. When you need a new word, you learn it. This ability explains why most people's vocabulary ceases growing after adolescence — they have fewer experiences that require them to learn new words. By age 5, most children have a vocabulary of about 4,000 words; by age 7, they know 20,000 words; and by age 10 they know 35,000. After that, the world isn't as new as it was before — kids have less to discover — and the average person's vocabulary grows at a much slower rate.

For example, consider the case of the woman who set out to become a gourmet cook. In the beginning, the names of cooking utensils like *zester, wok, lamé,* and *passatutto* were incomprehensible to her. After she got her hands on these utensils and used them in her kitchen, however, she could pass you the zester without blinking an eye. Absorbing these new words wasn't hard for her because she literally had hands-on experience with these cooking utensils, and knowing their names was necessary to her goal of becoming a gourmet cook.

Or consider what happens when you become ill. Because your health is at stake, you soon become intimately acquainted with hard-to-understand words from the medical profession that previously meant nothing to you. You want to master the words so you can intelligently discuss your health with your doctor, and you're soon able to throw these words around almost as well as your doctor can.

Discovering vocabulary words by context

You can also acquire new vocabulary words by context in the course of you reading. Whether you know it or not, you have a built-in aptitude for learning words by context. You don't have to consult a dictionary in your reading when you want to understand a new word. You learned new words by context when you first began to speak, and you certainly don't need to stop now. After all, no 3-year-old ever consults a dictionary, and yet a 3-year-old's vocabulary grows at a very fast clip.

When you come across a word you don't know, study it for a minute. See whether any part of it looks familiar. Perhaps you recognize a prefix, root, or suffix in the word that gives you a clue to its meaning (later in this chapter, "Looking at Prefixes, Roots, and Suffixes" explains what those elements are). Perhaps the sentence and paragraph where the word is found tell you what the word means.

Consider these sentences. Can you tell by context what the words in italics mean?

> The Bishop carried a large *crosier*. It was shaped like a shepherd's crook, only it was ornate and encrusted with jewels.

> The English dramatist W.S. Gilbert, who once remarked "I hate my fellow man," was a famous *misanthrope*.

> She loved to study, so much so that her friends started calling her a *bluestocking*.

> The amount of storage space on computers keeps getting larger. My first computer had only 15 kilobytes of storage. My next one had 20 gigabytes. Pretty soon we will measure storage in *terabytes* and *petabytes*.

The main point to remember about enlarging your vocabulary while you read is to not gloss over words you don't know. Pause in your reading and give them a moment's thought. You can't learn new words if you don't take the time to decode and absorb them.

To expand your vocabulary when reading, stretch your reading boundaries a little. As well as reading the metro section of the newspaper, for example, read the business section, where you can find business terminology and investment jargon you've never heard before. Read books outside your field of interest and scope of understanding. Next time you find yourself staring at the myriad of magazines on a magazine rack, choose a magazine you've never read before. Stray to obscure aisles of the library or bookstore and see what you discover.

Putting in a kind word for the dictionary

Don't hesitate to keep a dictionary nearby and consult it when you stumble upon a word you don't know. Circle each word you look up, and the pages of your dictionary soon fill with circled words. When you come across a circled word in the act of looking up a word definition, quiz yourself to see whether you understand the circled word's meaning.

You can also consult online dictionaries. Looking up a word online is often easier than looking it up in the pages of a fat, unwieldy book. Here are a few options:

✔ **American Heritage Dictionary:** www.bartleby.com/61/

✔ **Dictionary.com:** dictionary.reference.com/

✔ **Merriam-Webster:** www.merriam-webster.com/

✔ **Yourdictionary.com:** www.yourdictionary.com/

The Open Directory Project maintains a Web page with links to many different kinds of dictionaries, including foreign-language and specialty dictionaries. Head to www.dmoz.org//Reference/Dictionaries to check out this resource.

Looking at Prefixes, Roots, and Suffixes

One way to get a head start on expanding your vocabulary is to be able to recognize and interpret prefixes, roots, and suffixes in words. Many English words are constructed from the same prefixes, roots, and suffixes. Master these *affixes* (as linguists call them) and you can interpret many words you don't understand without having to resort to a dictionary.

For example, consider the word *neologism*. If you know this word's prefix, root, and suffix, you can understand its meaning without a dictionary:

✔ **neo:** This prefix means "new"; you can also find it in the words *Neolithic* and *neophyte*.

✔ **log:** This root means "word"; it also appears in the words *dialogue, epilogue,* and *monologue.*

✔ **ism:** This suffix indicates a condition or manner. It also shows up in the words *baptism* and *criticism*.

You can tell from decoding this word's prefix, root, and suffix that a *neologism* is (drum roll, please) a new word or phrase.

The following sections look at common prefixes, roots, and suffixes with the aim of helping you decode words as you read them and add words to your vocabulary. Get acquainted with these affixes; knowing their meanings can help you decipher most Greek- and Latin-derived words in a snap.

Peeking at prefixes

A *prefix* appears at the beginning of a word to give the word a new inflection or meaning. Table 12-1 lists common prefixes and their meanings and lists example words to help you understand what these prefixes do to words.

Table 12-1		Common Prefixes
Prefix	*Meaning*	*Example words*
a	not, lacking in	amoral, anachronism, anarchy, anemic, asexual, asymmetrical
ab	apart from	abdicate, abnormal, abduct
ante	before	antechamber, antedate, anteroom, antecedent
anti	against	anticlimax, antimatter, antipathy, antivirus
arch	supreme	archbishop, archenemy, archetype
auto	self	autobiography, autocrat, autoimmune, autosuggestion
be	beset with	becalm, beguile, bewildered, bewitch
bi	two	bicycle, biennial, binary, bipartisan, bisexual, bivalve
co	accompanying	cooperation, coordinator, coworker
contra	opposite	contraception, contradict, contralto, contravene
counter	in opposition	counteract, counterbalance, countermine, counterpart, counterpoint, counterterrorism
de	reverse	debrief, decompress, de-emphasize, deface
demi	half	demigod, demitasse, demimonde

(continued)

Table 12-1 *(continued)*

Prefix	Meaning	Example words
dis	opposite of	disagree, disenfranchise, disinherit, disloyal, disperse
en (em)	put into effect	empower, enforce, enlighten, envision
epi	on, over	epicenter, epidermis, epitaph, epithet
ex	out	exotic, exterior, extraneous, exoskeleton
fore	before	forecast, foreclose, foreplay, forerunner
in	not	inept, inexact, inhospitable
inter	between	interchangeable, interdict, interrelated, interact
ir	not	irrational, irrefutable, irregular, irrelevant
mal	badly	maladroit, malcontent, malnourished
micro	small	micromanage, microorganism, microscope
mid	middle	midday, midlife, midnight, midway
mis	wrong	misguided, misinformation, misplace
neo	new	neoclassic, neocolonial, neoconservative, neologism
non	not	noncommittal, nondescript, nonentity, nonexistent, non sequitur, nonstop
omni	all	omnibus, omnipotent, omnipresent, omniscient
out	beyond	outcast, outcome, outlaw, outplay, outreach
over	in excess of	overcharge, overhaul, overpower, overreact, overrun, overshoot, overstate
paleo	old	Paleolithic, Paleozoic
para	beside	paralegal, paraphrase, paraprofessional
per	completely	permeate, permutated
poly	many	polygamy, polyglot, polygon, Polynesian, polytheism

Prefix	Meaning	Example words
post	after	postgraduate, postmortem, postpone, postscript
pre	before	prefix, preview, prescient
quasi	partly	quasi-intelligent, quasi-happy
re	again	rekindle, rerun, revamp, revise
retro	backward	retroactive, retrofit, retrograde, restrospect
self	self	self-confident, self-defense, self-made, self-same, self-sufficient
semi	half	semicircle, semi-developed, semifinal, semi-naked
step	family relation	stepfather, stepmother, stepbrother, stepsister
sub	under, lesser	subconscious, subcommittee, subdue, submarine, subterranean
super	over, more	superhero, supernatural, superpower
syn	together	synchronize, syncopation, synthesis, synthetic
trans	across	transatlantic, transcontinental, transverse
ultra	extremely	ultracritical, ultraviolet, ultrared
un	not	ungrammatical, unmatched, unidentified, unencumbered, unnecessary, unprepared
under	below, less	underachieve, underclass, underdog, underground

Getting to the root of roots

Table 12-2 lists the most common word roots (also called *stems*) in the English language. These roots originate in Latin and ancient Greek. The table lists the meaning of each root and example words that show how the root plays out in different words.

Table 12-2		Common Roots
Root	*Meaning*	*Example words*
acer	bitter, sour	acerbic, acrimony
acu	sharp	accurate, acute
ag	do, go	agenda, agent
alt	height	altimeter, altitude
alter	other	alter ego, alternate, alternative
ami (amor)	love, friendship	amiable, amicable, amorous, enamored
amphi	both	amphibian, amphibious
ann (enni)	year	anniversary, annual, biennial, centennial, perennial
anthrop	human	anthropology, misanthrope, philanthropy
anti	old	antique, antiquated
aqua	water	aquatic, aquarium, aqueduct
arch	first, ruler	archaic, archangel, matriarch, monarch, patriarch
arthro	joint	arthritis, arthroscopic
aster	star	asterisk, asteroid, astronomy
aud	listen	audible, audiotape, auditory, auditorium
bell	war	bellicose, belligerent, rebel, rebellion
biblio	book	bible, bibliography, bibliophile
bio	life	antibiotic, biography, biology, biometrics
brev	short	abbreviate, brief
calor	heat	caloric, calorie
cap (cep)	take, seize	capable, captivate, capacity, capture, forceps, intercept
carn	flesh	carnal, carnivorous, chili con carne, incarnate, reincarnation
caus	burn	cauldron, caustic, cauterize

Root	Meaning	Example words
ced	yield, go	accede, cede, concede, intercede, proceed, recede
chrom	color	chromatic, monochrome, polychrome
chron	time	chronicle, chronology, chronometer, synchronize
cide	kill	homicide, germicide, patricide, suicide
cit	call, start	cite, citation, incite
civ	citizen	civil, civilian, civilization
clam	cry out	acclaim, clamor, exclamation, proclaim
cogn	know	cognitive, cognoscenti, incognito, recognize
cord (cour)	heart	cordial, courage, discord, encourage
corp	body	corporal, corporation, corpse, corpulent
cosm	universe	cosmopolitan, cosmos, microcosm
cracy (crat)	rule, ruler	autocrat, bureaucrat, democracy, theocracy
cred	belief	credible, credulous, credibility, credit, credo, creed, incredible
cruc	cross	crucifix, crucial, crux
crypt	hidden	crypt, cryptic, cryptogram
culp	guilt	culpable, culprit
cura	care	curator, curative, manicure, pedicure
curs	run, happen	concur, current, incur, occur, recur
deca	ten	decade, decathlon, decimate
dei	god	deify, deity
demo	people	democracy, demographics, epidemic, pandemic
dent (dont)	teeth	dental, dentist, orthodontist
derm	skin	dermatology, epidermis, hypodermic, taxidermy

(continued)

Table 12-2 *(continued)*

Root	Meaning	Example words
dict	say, speak	benediction, dictate, dictionary, indict, predict, verdict
doc	teach	doctrine, document, indoctrinate
dom	master	domain, dominate, dominion
dorm	sleep	dormant, dormitory
dox	belief	heterodoxy, orthodox, paradox
duc (duct)	lead	abduct, conduct, deduce, induce, reduce, seduction
duo	two	dual, duet, duo, duopoly
dur	hard, difficult	durable, duration, endure
dynam	power	dynamic, dynamite, dynamo
endo	inside	endoskeleton, endosperm
equ	equal	equal, equanimity, equate, equity, equidistant
ex	out	exterior, exterior, extraneous, exoskeleton
fac (fect, fic)	make, do	benefactor, factory, manufacture
fer	carry	defer, ferry, infer, refer, transfer
fid	faithful	confidante, fidelity, Fido, infidel
fin	finish	final, finale, finish, finite
fix	attach	affix, fixate, fixture, prefix, suffix
flex (flect)	bend	deflect, flexible, inflexible, reflect
flu (fluc)	flow	fluent, fluid, fluctuate
form	shape	conform, form, uniform
fort	strength	fort, forte, fortify, fortitude
frag (fract)	break	fraction, fracture, infraction, refract
frater	brother	fraternal, fraternity, fraternize

Root	Meaning	Example words
gam	marriage	bigamy, monogamy, polygamy
gastro	stomach	gastric, gastritis, gastronomic
gen	people	eugenics, genetic, genealogy
geo	earth	geography, geology, geometry, geopolitical, geothermal
grad (gress)	step	grade, gradual, graduate, transgression
graph (gram)	write, writing	autograph, biography, geography, graphic, photography, pornography, telegraph
grav	heavy	gravitate, gravity
greg	herd	congregation, gregarious, segregate
helio	sun	heliograph, heliotrope
hemo	blood	hemophilia, hematology, hemoglobin
here (hes)	stick	adhere, cohere, cohesion, hereditary
hetero	different	heterogeneous, heterosexual, heterodox
homo	same	homogenize, homogenous, homonym, homosexual
hydr	water	dehydrate, hydrant, hydraulics, hydroelectric
ignis	fire	igneous, ignite, ignition
ject	throw	deject, inject, interject, project, reject, subject
jud	judge	adjudicate, judicial, judge
juven	youth	juvenile, rejuvenate
lav (lau, lot, luv)	wash	ablution, launder, lavatory, lotion
lect	read	lectern, lecturer, legible
leg	law	election, legal, legislate, legitimate
levi	lighten	alleviate, levitate, levity
liber	free	liberal, liberate, liberty

(continued)

Table 12-2 *(continued)*

Root	Meaning	Example words
liter	letter	alliteration, illiterate, literal, literature
loc	place	allocate, local, location
log	word	dialogue, epilogue, logo, monologue, prologue
loqu (locut)	speak	colloquial, eloquent, loquacious
luc	light	elucidate, lucid, pellucid
magn	great	magnanimous, magnate, magnificent, magnify, magnitude
man	hand	manage, manicure, manual, manufacture, manuscript
mand	command	mandate, mandatory, remand
mania	madness	kleptomania, mania, maniac, pyromania
mar (mari, meri)	sea	marine, mariner, maritime, mermaid
matri (mater)	mother	maternal, maternity, matriarchy, matron
medi	half	mediate, medieval, mediocre, medium
mega	large	megacycle, megalopolis, megaphone
mem	remembrance	memento, memo, memorable, memoir, memory, remember
metri (meter)	measure	barometer, geometric, metric system, odometer, thermometer
micro	tiny	microfilm, microscope, microwave
migra	wander	emigrant, immigration, migrate
min	small	minority, minuscule, minute
mit (miss)	send	emit, missile, mission, permit, remit, submit, transmit
mob (mot, mov)	move	automobile, mobile, motion, promote, movie
mon	warning	admonition, monitor, premonition

Root	Meaning	Example words
mono	one	monochromatic, monogamy, monopoly, monotheism
mor (mort)	death	immortality, morbid, moribund, mortal, mortician, mortuary
morph	change	amorphous, metamorphosis, morph, morphology
multi	many	multifold, multiply, multitude
mut	mutate	mutability, mutant, mutate
nat (nasc)	begin, be born	innate, natal, native, renaissance
neo	new	Neocene, neocortex, neolithic, neophyte
neur	nerve	neurology, neurosis, neurobiology
nom	name	nomenclature, nominal, nominate
nov	new	innovation, novel, nova, novice, renovate
numer	number	enumerate, innumerable, number, numeral
nym	name	acronym, anonymous, pseudonym, synonym
ortho	straight	orthodontist, orthodox, orthopedic
pac	peace	pacifist, pacify, Pacific Ocean
pan	all	panacea, panorama, panegyric
pater	father	paternal, paternity, patricide, patrilineal, patriotic, patron
pathy	feeling	apathy, empathy, pathology, sympathy, telepathy
ped (pod)	foot	centipede, orthopedic, pedal, pedestrian, pedometer, podiatry, tripod
pedo	child	pediatrics, pedophile
pel (puls)	push, urge	compel, dispel, expel, impulse, propel, pulse, pulsate, repel, repulsive

(continued)

Table 12-2 *(continued)*

Root	Meaning	Example words
pend	hang, weigh	appendage, pending, pendulum, suspend
phil	love	anglophile, bibliophile, philanthropy, philosophy
phobia	fear	claustrophobia, homophobia, phobia
phon	sound	cacophony, euphony, homophone, phonetic, phonograph, symphony, telephone
plac	please	complacent, placebo, placate, placid
plan	flat	planar, plantation, plane
plu	more	plural, plus
pneum	lung	pneumatic, pneumonia
poli	city	Indianapolis, megalopolis, metropolitan, police
pop	people	population, populous, popular
port	carry	export, import, portable, porter, report, support, transportation
pot	power	omnipotent, potent, potentate
prehend	grasp, seize	apprehend, comprehend, comprehensive, prehensile
prim	first	primacy, primal, primary, primitive, primo
psych	soul, mind	psyche, psychic, psychology, psychosis
pugna	fight	pugnacious, pugilist
punct	point	acupuncture, puncture, punctual, punctuation
quer (quis)	ask	query, inquisition
reg (rect)	straighten	correct, direct, rectangle, rectify
ris (rid)	laugh	deride, ridicule, ridiculous, risible
rupt	break	abrupt, disrupt, interrupt, rupture
sacr (sanc)	holy	consecrate, desecrate, sacred, sacrosanct

Root	Meaning	Example words
sat (satis)	enough	sate, satisfy, saturate
scent (scend)	climb	ascend, ascent, descend, descent
sci (scientia)	knowledge	conscience, omniscient, science, scientific
scrib (script)	write	describe, inscribe, manuscript, prescribe, scribe, scribble, scripture
sec	cut	dissect, section
sen	old	senator, senescence, senile, senior
sens (sent)	feel	consent, dissent, resent, sensible, sense, sensation, sensitive, sentiment
sequ (secu)	follow	consecutive, consequence, second, sequence, sequel
serv	serve, protect	conserve, reserve, servant, service, servitude
sign	sign, mark	design, insignia, signature, signal, significant
simil	similar	assimilate, facsimile (fax), similar, simile, simultaneous, simulate
solus	alone	solitary, solitude, soliloquy, solo
son	sound	resonate, sonar, unison
soph	wisdom	philosophy, sophisticated, sophomore
spec (spic)	look	aspect, conspicuous, inauspicious, inspect, introspective, prospect, retrospective, spectacles, spectator
spir	breath	conspire, expire, inspire, respiration
string (strict)	tighten	constrict, restrict, strict, stringent
stru (struct)	build	construct, destruction, instruct, obstruct, structure
tang (tact)	touch	contact, contagious, intact, intangible, tactile, tangible

(continued)

Table 12-2 *(continued)*

Root	Meaning	Example words
tele	far	telecast, telephone, telescope, telepathy, television
temp	time	contemporary, extemporaneously, tempo, temporal, temporary
ten	hold	detention, retentive, tenable, tentative, tenuous, untenable
tend	stretch	content, extend, intend, pretend, tension
terra (ter)	earth	disinter, subterranean, terrain, terrestrial, territory
test	bear witness	attest, detest, testify, testimony
theo (the)	god	atheist, polytheism, monotheist, theology
therm	heat	hypothermia, thermos, thermometer, thermostat
tor	twist	contort, distort, extort, retort, torture, torturous
tox	poison	detox, intoxicate, toxic
tract (tra)	pull	attract, subtract, traction, tractor
trib	bestow	attribute, contribute, retribution, tribute
turb (turm)	disturb	disturb, turbulent, turmoil
typ	print	prototype, type, typography, typology
umber	shadow	penumbra, umbra, umbrella
uni	one	unanimous, unicorn, unify, universal
vac	empty	evacuate, vacant, vacation, vacuous, vacuum
val	strength	equivalent, valiant, valor, value
ven (vent)	come	avenue, convene, intervene, prevent, venture
ver	truth	aver, veracity, verdict, verify, verity, very, verisimilitude

Root	Meaning	Example words
vert (vers)	turn	avert, convertible, divert, irreversible, introvert, reverse, versatile
vict (vinc)	conquer	convict, convince, evict, invincible, victor
vid (vis)	see	evident, revise, video, visible, vision, vista
viv (vita, vivi)	life	revitalize, survive, vital, vitamin, vitality, vivacious
voc	call	convocation, evocative, invocation, provoke, revoke, vocal
volvo	roll	evolve, evolution, revolve, revolution
vor	eat	devour, carnivorous, herbivorous, omnivore, voracious
zo	animal	zoo, zoology, zoolatry

Searching out suffixes

A _suffix_ appears at the end of a word and gives the word a different inflection or meaning. Table 12-3 gives you some common suffixes, plus their meanings and examples of them in action.

Table 12-3		Common Suffixes
Suffix	Meaning	Example words
able (ible)	capable of	agreeable, capable, manageable, solvable, visible
ade	result of an action	blockade, stockade
age	result of	courage, spillage, storage, stoppage, wreckage, wastage
al (ial)	relating to	categorical, gradual, manual, referral, territorial
algia	sickness	myalgia, neuralgia, nostalgia
an	native of or to	American, African, artisan, Cartesian, European

(continued)

Table 12-3 *(continued)*

Root	Meaning	Example words
ance (ence)	state	assistance, defiance, independence, resistance
ancy (ency)	capacity	agency, vacancy
ate	office	candidate, graduate, potentate
ation	state	matriculation, specialization
cian	having a skill	magician, physician
cy	action	infancy, normalcy, privacy, prophecy
dom	quality	freedom, kingdom, wisdom
ee	person receiving action	nominee, refugee
en	made of	frozen, molten, silken, waxen
er	comparative	brighter, cleaner, happier, tougher
er (or)	doer	boxer, collector, lover, professor
escene	in process	adolescence, obsolescence
ese	native of	Chinese, Japanese
esis (osis)	in process	hypnosis, neurosis, osmosis
est	superlative	brightest, cleanest, fastest, happiest
et (ette)	small	anklet, baguette
fic	causing	horrific, terrific
fold	manner of	manifold, tenfold
ful	full of	bountiful, fanciful, helpful, mindful, mouthful
fy	making	deify, indemnify, rectify, simplify
hood	condition	adulthood, childhood, manhood
ian	one who is	pedestrian
iatry	healing	podiatry, psychiatry

Root	Meaning	Example words
ic	quality of	acidic, metallic, monolithic
ic	arts, sciences	arithmetic, economics
ice	condition	justice, malice
ile	quality	domicile, juvenile, projectile
ion	condition	abduction
ish	comparative	British, foolish, newish, whitish
ism	condition	alcoholism, baptism, neologism
ist	profession	artist, dentist, podiatrist
ite	quality	anchorite, socialite, urbanite
ity (ty)	quality	celebrity, clarity, lucidity, novelty
ive	quality	abusive, cooperative, festive, sensitive
ize	cause, make	emphasize, fantasize, idolize, proselytize
less	without	loveless, mindless, motionless
ment	state	abatement, contentment, refinement
ness	quality	calmness, kindness, tenderness
ology	study of	biology, geology, neurology
ous	quality	adventurous, courageous, fractious, nervous
ship	relationship	brinksmanship, friendship, one-upmanship
some	quality	adventuresome, lonesome, winsome
ure	condition	culture, conjecture, exposure, rapture
ward	direction	forward, heavenward, northward, southward
y	tending to	crafty, faulty

Chapter 13

Applying Speed Reading to Various Reading Tasks

*T*his chapter explores reading challenges and strategies that come with common reading tasks such as keeping up with the news and dealing with a flood of e-mail. It also gives advice for readers faced with daunting nonfiction books or textbooks. You also discover tips for nailing standardized tests.

 Though I don't specifically mention all kinds of literature and communication here, you can use the strategies in this chapter (and throughout this book) to speed read magazines, memos, sales reports, trade journals, medical articles — the list is endless.

Speed Reading the Newspaper

Newspapers are built for speed reading. The newspaper is divided into sections — news, sports, business, and so on — to help you quickly locate articles that interest you. On the front page, the article that the editors deem most important occupies the upper-right columns; the second most important article appears in the upper-left columns. Some articles have subheadings that spell out what information is available. In news articles, facts are presented in descending order of importance so that you can get the gist of a story by reading the first one or two paragraphs and then keep reading if you decide you want to know more. The narrow columns help with reading speed because they encourage you to take in the five to seven words that span each column with a single eye fixation, and that increases your reading speed.

That doesn't mean you can go full blast whenever you read the newspaper. You have to slow down from time to time, depending on the type of article you're reading:

✔ **Fact reporting:** You can read articles that report bare facts — like the kind that are found on the first page — quickly. These articles explain the how, where, who, when, and why. You can speed read this information.

✔ **Explanation:** Slow down when you encounter an article that attempts to explain the news. These articles offer opinion as well as fact, so you have to take extra time to distinguish the author's opinions from fact and read the opinions with a critical eye.

✔ **Opinion:** Read opinion pieces like the kind found on the op-ed page slowly. These articles aren't structured like the other articles in the newspaper. In an opinion piece, the author constructs an argument, and you have to mind how the argument unfolds to see whether you agree with it. Because opinion pieces are subjective, you have to read them skeptically (and perhaps seek out opposing views as well). This practice requires more reading time.

Finding news to speed read online

Here are some good online places to look for news about your favorite topic:

✔ **All the Web News** (`www.alltheweb.com/?cat=news`): Search for news by keyword or click the Advanced Search link to search for news by category.

✔ **Alta Vista News** (`news.altavista.com`): Search for news by keyword. You can make choices on the Topic, Region, and Date Range drop-down menus to direct your search.

✔ **Google News** (`news.google.com`): Search for news by keyword in 4,500 news sources or by browsing in different categories.

✔ **World News Network** (`www.wn.com`): Search in news sources outside the United States.

✔ **Yahoo! News** (`news.yahoo.com`): Search for news by keyword or by browsing in different categories for stories collected by Yahoo! editors.

By the way, you can locate any newspaper's home page from the Metagrid Web site. Its address is `www.metagrid.com`

Be extra alert when the author of a newspaper article ventures his or her opinion in a fact-reporting or explanation article. In these articles, determining whether you're reading a fact or an opinion is difficult. By necessity, you have to read more slowly in these cases to separate facts from opinions.

Managing Online Articles

Many people do the majority of their reading on the Internet. Where speed reading is concerned, the same basic rules apply to reading online and reading words printed on good old-fashioned paper. Reading online, however, has a couple of advantages and disadvantages.

The advantages of reading online have to do with being able to manipulate the appearance of text. You can use commands in your Web browser to enlarge or shrink the text and make reading more comfortable for you. (In Internet Explorer, choose View⇨Text Size and select an option on the submenu; in Mozilla Firefox, choose View⇨Zoom In or Zoom Out.) You can also enlarge the Web page you are reading to full-screen size (press F11). At full-screen size, the Web browser menus and toolbars are hidden, which makes it easier to focus on the text. (Press F11 again to display menus and toolbars).

The disadvantages of reading online all boil down to one central problem — it's harder to focus and concentrate when reading online, and focusing and concentrating with more force of will is a basic principle of speed reading.

Tips for reading computer screen text

Reading lots of text on a computer screen can be uncomfortable, but these helpful hints make computer reading less of a strain on your eyes. Make sure your monitor is in the proper light. If you're using a flat-screen LCD monitor, put it in direct light. LCD monitors are sidelit or backlit, and they're easier to see in full lighting. If you're using an old-fashioned CRT monitor (one of those bulky jobs that weighs a ton), keep the monitor out of direct light to prevent glare.

Try experimenting with the knobs and controls on your monitor. Twist and turn them until you find a look for the screen that is comfortable for your eyes. And you can adjust your Web browser to shrink and enlarge the text on-screen. Check out "Managing Online Articles" in this chapter for directions.

Think of all the distractions and temptations you're subject to when you're online. If you start to get bored, you can always go to a different page or site, and you can get there faster than you can snap your fingers. Hyperlinks in the text all cry out for you to click them and go elsewhere. Some Web pages play music or sound, which can be a distraction. Have you checked your e-mail lately? Maybe somebody you want to hear from has written you.

You have to redouble your efforts at concentration when you speed read online. Bear down and really focus on what you're reading. Pretend that you're reading from a printed page. That way, you aren't as tempted by the many distractions of the Internet.

Handling E-mail Correspondence

If you're one of those unfortunate souls who receives 30, 40, 50, or more e-mail messages daily, you owe it to yourself and your sanity to figure out a scheme for speed reading, prioritizing, and storing all that e-mail.

You can read most e-mail messages quickly because e-mail messages are by nature short and to the point. As for long e-mails, use the same speed-reading techniques you use, for example, to read an essay, and don't be afraid to scan and skim (check out Chapter 10).

Just remember that all e-mail programs offer you the opportunity to choose a font and font size that make reading e-mail easier. If you read your e-mail in a Web-based program such as Google Mail, you can change the size of e-mail text by changing the text size setting in your Web browser (see the preceding section for resizing details). If you read your e-mail in a program such as Outlook 2007, look for the menu commands that control the font and font size of text and experiment with them until you find a font and font size that makes reading the messages easier.

A place for everything

You can't speed read an old e-mail if you can't find it. To prioritize and sort e-mail, set up a folder scheme for storing the mail and place e-mail messages in the correct folders after you read them. For example, create and name an e-mail folder for each project you're working on and then shunt e-mail messages into the project folders as you finish reading them. This strategy makes it easier for you to locate and reply to e-mail messages.

You can save time by weeding out mail that doesn't need reading in the first place. When you check your e-mail, start by deleting all messages that don't matter to you. If your e-mail program has a spam filter, use it. Spam filters prevent junk e-mail from arriving in your inbox to torture you.

Prereading Nonfiction Books

It's true — you can't judge a book by its cover. But you can tell a lot about a nonfiction book by *prereading* it, or examining the particulars before you read the first page. (Check out Chapter 10 for more on the art of prereading.). By prereading, you can tell what information is in the book and whether reading part or all of it is worthwhile.

Examine these parts of a book before you read it:

- ✔ **Table of contents:** Glance at the chapter titles and headings to find out what's in the book. You can also tell a lot about an author's ability to organize ideas and present arguments from the table of contents. If the topics in the table of contents are presented in a logical manner, if each topic leads succinctly into the next, you're holding a well-organized book in your hands.

- ✔ **Index:** Scour the index for information about the topic you're interested in. If the information you need isn't in the index, the book probably isn't worth reading.

- ✔ **Preface:** You can usually find a good description of the book's purpose in the preface, as well as information about the author's background and credentials.

- ✔ **Introduction:** A good introduction explains what is covered in the book. Plus, you can get a feel for the author's writing and determine whether the book will be easy to read or a slog.

- ✔ **Chapter summaries:** Find out whether the last paragraph of each chapter offers a summary of the chapter; if it does, read those last paragraphs first. You can get a rock-solid idea of what the book covers this way.

 While you're examining your nonfiction book, take a look at the copyright page to see when it was published. If the book covers a subject that has undergone changes in recent years, the book may be out of date and not useful to you. The copyright page is located on the flipside of the title page.

Tackling Textbooks

I'm guessing that if you have to read a textbook, you have no choice in the matter because a teacher or professor assigned it to you. I bet your textbook is many pages long and would crush your big toe if you happened to drop it there. And I imagine your instructor assigns many pages as though you have nothing else to do with your time, and you want some advice about speed reading them so that you can go out (or, you know, get some sleep) later.

Earlier in this chapter, "Prereading nonfiction books" explains how to examine a book to find out what information it offers before you begin reading. The prereading advice for examining nonfiction books also applies to textbooks. Here are some specific tips for reading textbooks quickly:

- ✔ **Read the glossary first (if your textbook has one).** Taking the time to acquire words you don't know from the glossary is worthwhile because it enables you to read the textbook that much more quickly when the time comes to start reading.

- ✔ **Scour the pages for graphs, charts, and tables.** Especially in science textbooks, graphs, charts, and tables sometimes tell half the story. Acquainting yourself with these items is an excellent way to get a feel for the information that the textbook has to offer.

- ✔ **Find out what your teacher or professor wants you to learn from the textbook and seek out that info.** No sense in slaving over text you're not accountable for. Plus, you probably paid a small fortune for that textbook; your teacher or professor owes you an explanation about what to read in it.

- ✔ **Develop an underlining or note-taking scheme and mark the textbook as you read.** My favorite note-taking technique is to draw a dot next to passages in the book that I think are important or worth reviewing. Later, I can quickly scan for these important passages. (See Chapter 10 for more on scanning.)

- ✔ **Improve retention by reviewing and quizzing yourself.** When you finish reading a chapter or selection, pause a moment and summarize to yourself what you just read. Make up half a dozen questions about the material and then answer them. This technique helps you retain what you read. Retention matters more than usual when reading textbooks because you're usually quizzed or tested about textbook material. And though this practice takes a bit more time initially, it actually saves you time in the long run because you don't spend as much time rereading later.

Helping your child become a speedy reader

To become a speed reader, one of your first challenges is to stop *vocalizing* when you read. If you say the words when you read, you can't read quickly because saying words to yourself takes time — time you can use to speed ahead with your reading.

Most people vocalize because that's how they learned to read. In the learn-to-read phase, first, second, and third graders learn to sound out words by recognizing letter combinations on the page and speaking these combinations as sounds in the act of reading.

If you want your child to become a speed reader (or at least a better reader), your first task is to discourage the vocalization habit. Starting in the third or fourth grade, have your child concentrate on reading without vocalizing. Tell him to see and read more than one word at a time and process the words without sounding them out.

If your child continues to move his lips in the act of reading, have him chew gum, hold a finger over his closed lips, or hold a pencil in his lips while reading. Present this correction as a fun activity for your child to engage in, and he'll quickly break the vocalization habit.

Studies show that children from households where parents and other family members read are better readers than other children. These children understand that reading is a pleasurable activity, not an onerous chore. Make books and reading a part of your family's daily life if you want your child to read well. If you have young children who aren't of reading age, read to them on a regular basis. It will give them a big head start when it comes time for them to read on their own.

Speed Reading Standardized Tests

Here's a little-known fact that can help you immensely when you take a standardized test such as the SAT, LSAT, or a driver's license exam: Every standardized test is really a speed-reading test.

Standardized tests don't measure what you know as much as they measure how well you can apply logic and reason to different topics. If you can read the questions and test material more quickly, you get more time to think through to the right answers. A standardized test measures how much time you give yourself to think, and if you can speed read, you get more time for thinking.

To test my theory, try this experiment: Next time you watch a TV quiz show such as *Jeopardy!* that requires you to read questions, try applying speed-reading techniques to your reading. You'll read the questions faster, get more time to find the answers, and discover that you answer the questions correctly more often. You can apply the extra time you gain by speed reading to rummaging in your brain for the right answer.

Here are some tips for taking standardized tests:

✔ **Preread the test before you answer any questions.** No cheating; wait until your allotted time begins, of course. Find out which parts of the test are easiest for you and answer the questions in those parts of the test first. If time is a factor in taking the test and you believe you can't answer all the questions, answering the easiest questions guarantees you a higher score.

✔ **Speed read the test's reading comprehension questions before you read the selection text.** In other words, if the reading selection is "The History of Ohio," read the questions about Ohio history before reading the essay. This way, you know what to look for in the text as you read and you can skim or skip reading material you aren't tested on.

✔ **Know how the test is scored.** If you know which parts of the test matter most to your score, you can focus on those parts and improve your score.

✔ **Adopt the speed-reading mindset during the test.** Read aggressively and hungrily. Focus like a laser beam on the page in front of you and concentrate with all your might. Speed reading improves not only reading skills but also concentration skills.

Reading for Pleasure

In all the talk of reading efficiency and reading speed, you can easily forget that reading is one of life's greatest pleasures. And because it's so pleasurable, savor the reading experience when you feel the urge. Slow down and enjoy the novels, biographies, math treatises, history books, or whatever type of books you love most.

Don't hesitate to throw aside the rules of speed reading from time to time if doing so increases your reading pleasure. When reading poetry, you want to vocalize. You want to hear and revel in the sounds of the words. Reading the speeches of the great orators is much more rewarding when you slow down to hear the words. Make your own rules when it comes to pleasure reading. You can slow down or speed up, vocalize or not, as you please.

My hope is that discovering how to speed read allows you to get your obligatory reading done more quickly so you can get to your pleasure reading sooner.

Part V
The Part of Tens

The 5th Wave   By Rich Tennant

"...and how long have you been practicing these speed reading techniques?"

In this part...

*E*ach chapter in Part V offers ten tidbits of good, rock-solid advice for being a better speed reader. With three chapters in this part, that makes 30 — count 'em, 30 — tidbits in all.

Chapter 14 gives you suggestions for improving your speed reading. Chapter 15 helps you widen your reading vision, and Chapter 16 tackles tips for making your speed-reading skills permanent.

Chapter 14

Ten Quick Techniques to Improve Your Reading Speed

This part of tens chapter offers — count 'em — ten fundamental techniques for improving your reading speed. These suggestions represent the basics of speed reading. You can adopt these techniques and get a big head start in your speed reading adventures.

Make the Speed-Reading Commitment

Half the task of becoming a speed reader is making a commitment to read faster. By now you've spent quite a bit of time as a reader, and you've probably fallen into some slow reading habits. You're used to hearing the words as you read them or regress or dawdle when you read. You don't go at it conscientiously with the goal of getting as much meaning as you can from your reading. To be a speed reader, you must renounce slow reading habits and make the commitment to reading in an entirely different way.

Focus Like a Laser Beam

Speed reading requires more brainpower, concentration, and determination on the reader's part. To speed read, you must focus intensely — and not just on the author's words. As well as taking in the words, you have to be attuned to the flow of ideas and the author's strategies for presenting his or her argument. You distinguish between the main ideas and the details as you read. You're aware of your reading goals and, to meet those goals, you decide when to slow down and speed up in the course of your reading. (See "Vary Your Reading Rate" later in this chapter for more on when to change up your speed.)

See It, Don't Say It

In the act of reading, most people *vocalize* (hear the words as they see them on the page). But vocalizing slows you down, so seeing words without hearing them is an essential skill if you want to be a speed reader.

To keep from hearing words when you read, turn off your ears. Try to squelch your inner voice. If you move your lips when you read, try chewing gum or placing a pen or pencil between your lips. Occupying your mouth and lips while you read prevents you from moving your lips — and from hearing the words as you read them. Head to Chapter 2 for more on vocalizing and how to stop it.

Resist the Regression Urge

Regression is the term reading educators use for *rereading*. People regress for different reasons, but whatever the cause, it slows down reading and lowers comprehension. (Chapter 2 gives you the lowdown on the causes of regression.)

To prevent yourself from regressing, resist the urge. When you feel the need to reread, just keep chugging along. You may be surprised to discover that rereading isn't as necessary as you thought, and you'll develop more confidence in your reading and find yourself regressing less and less.

Widen Your Vision Span

A primary goal of speed reading is to be able to read many words at once. To accomplish this feat, you must widen your *vision span* (the number of words you can read horizontally and vertically on a page). The more words you can see and understand at once, the faster you can read.

A good speed reader can take in 10 to 14 words at a time. In your reading, get in the habit of taking in four or more words at a stretch. You can do that by seeing and processing the words as images, not as sounds, and by literally widening your vision. Instead of reading word by word, try to read phrase by phrase or sentence by sentence.

Preread It

Before visiting a foreign country, most people consult a guidebook to decide what to visit. The guidebook gives them the flavor of the country and points them to outstanding places that are worth visiting. Similarly, you can increase your reading speed by *prereading* your document (looking at its landmarks before you start reading it). If you're reading a book, glance at the table of contents and index. If you're reading an article, read the headings, subheadings, captions, pull quotes, graphs, and charts first.

Prereading helps you set your reading goals and points you to the areas of interest. Maybe only a few parts of an article are worth your time — prereading helps you locate these parts.

Vary Your Reading Rate

Just because you're a supersonic speed reader doesn't mean you always read at lightning speed. Part of being a speed reader is understanding when to slow down and when to speed up.

When you get stuck in traffic or find yourself on a slick stretch of highway, you slow down for safety's sake to make sure you have better control of your car. The same is true of reading. When you come to a hard-to-understand passage or a paragraph that requires more than the usual amount of attention, slow down a bit. Reading isn't the act of seeing words on the page but rather the act of comprehending the words, and sometimes slowing down is necessary for comprehension.

And when you come to a passage or paragraph that doesn't require as much attention, go full speed ahead.

Read for the Main Ideas

You can't be a speed reader *and* a stickler for details. Too much attention to detail or a reverence for minor arguments can keep you from quickly recognizing and comprehending the author's main ideas or themes. In your reading, see whether you can sense how the material you're reading is structured around its main theme or idea, and when you find where that theme or idea is located, pounce on it. Your goal is to get the gist of what the author is saying, not get the flavor of all the details.

Use the Eye Sweep

When you come to the end of one line in your reading and need to go to the next line, don't dawdle — quickly sweep your eyes to the next line. This practice increases your reading speed and reinforces the sense of urgency you need when speed reading.

In the beginning of your training, you may use a pacer to facilitate going quickly and directly to the next line. However, I don't recommend using a pacer for long; you can get in the habit of eye sweeping soon enough without having to use the pacer for long.

Get Your Eyes Checked

This last one isn't really a technique, but it's important if you want to be a speed reader. The eyes, besides being the windows of the soul, are also the windows through which you read, and you can't see very much if the windows are dirty. Your eyes need to be in good working order for you to reach your speed-reading potential.

When was the last time you had your eyes checked or were fitted for a new pair of glasses? Visit your optometrist to make sure your eyes are fully prepared to help you in your speed reading.

Chapter 15

Ten Exercises for Keeping Your Eyes Speed-Reading Ready

In This Chapter

▶ Strengthening your eyes

▶ Making your eye muscles more flexible

▶ Resting your peepers

*E*yesight is controlled by muscles in your eye sockets and eyeballs, and like the rest of your muscles, you can strengthen them through exercise. Eye strength comes in handy for speed reading, which taxes your eyes more than regular reading because it requires your eyes to cover more distance on the page. By making your eye muscles stronger and more flexible, you can improve your clarity of vision and slow down the natural eyesight deterioration that occurs with aging.

This chapter presents ten eye exercises to improve your eye health and, by connection, your speed reading. These exercises help you strengthen, rest, and make your eye muscles more flexible so that your eyes can jump quickly across the page and you can be a better speed reader.

Eye Squeezes

Doing eye squeezes relaxes your eyes, makes your eye muscles more flexible, and increases the flow of blood and oxygen to your eyes and face. This exercise takes about three minutes:

1. **As you inhale deeply and slowly, open your eyes and mouth as wide as you can and stretch out all the muscles of your face.**

2. As you exhale, close and squeeze your eyes as tightly as you can while also squeezing all the muscles of your face, neck, and head and clenching your jaws.

3. Hold your breath and continue squeezing for 30 seconds.

4. Repeat Steps 1 through 3 four more times, take a short break, and then do another set of five squeezes.

Don't attempt eye squeezes in an office or other location where other people can see you. Your eyes are closed during part of this exercise, so trust me when I say that you look awfully strange while you're doing it.

Thumb-to-Thumb Glancing

Thumb-to-thumb glancing works the muscles in your eye sockets that control peripheral vision and stretches the eye muscles in general to make them healthier and more flexible.

To get the most from this exercise, try to glance at your thumbs without moving your head.

1. Sitting or standing, look straight ahead, stretch your arms out to your sides, and stick up your thumbs.

2. Without turning your head, glance back and forth between your left and right thumbs ten times.

3. Repeat Steps 1 and 2 three times.

Tree Pose

The tree pose is a yoga balancing exercise that's essentially a more advanced version of thumb-to-thumb glancing (covered in the preceding section). It works your peripheral vision and makes your eye muscles more flexible. You can't cheat on this exercise (not that you'd try) because if you do it incorrectly, you'll topple over. The tree pose exercise takes about five minutes, including resting time between sets.

Do this exercise standing beside a chair or table — something you can grab onto if you start to fall.

1. Stand with your feet shoulder width apart and stare at a fixed point eight or ten feet in front of your nose.

2. Raise your hands and press your palms together at chest level.

3. **Maintaining your balance, slowly raise your left foot to knee level.**

   Or, if you want to make like a true yogi, place your left foot on your inner right thigh.

4. **Without moving your head, turn your eyes as far as you can to the left and focus on an object in the farthest corner of your left-hand field of vision and then do the same to your right.**

   If you move your head, you'll lose your balance.

5. **Repeat Step 4 for 30 seconds, maintaining the balanced position, and then lower your left foot to the ground.**

6. **Repeat Steps 1 through 5, raising your right foot and balancing on your left.**

Do three sets, standing on your left and right foot for each set.

Eye Rolling

The next time someone rolls his eyes at you, don't get angry — congratulate him for giving his eyes a workout. As an exercise, eye rolling strengthens the extra-ocular muscles of the eye socket that control the position of the eyeball and makes your eyes more flexible.

Instead of finding exasperating occasions to roll your eyes, try the following exercise, which only takes about a minute.

1. **Sit looking straight ahead.**

2. **Roll your eyes clockwise and blink.**

3. **Roll your eyes counterclockwise and blink.**

4. **Repeat Steps 2 and 3 five times.**

Eye Writing

This exercise gets you to move your eyes in ways unrelated to normal seeing, which gives them a good workout. Like eye rolling (discussed in the preceding section), eye writing exercises the extra-ocular muscles of the eye socket and is especially good for increasing the eyeball's flexibility and range of motion. Eye writing couldn't be simpler:

1. **Look at the wall on the other side of the room (or the wall that is farthest away from you).**

2. **Imagine that you're writing your name on the wall with your eyes.**

   In other words, move your eyes as you would move a paintbrush if you were painting the letters of your name on the wall. Try writing your name in block letters and then in cursive letters. Write your name large. Be sure to dot your *i*'s and cross your *t*'s.

The 10-10-10

This exercise is called the 10-10-10 because it asks you to stare at an object that is ten or more feet away for ten seconds every ten minutes when you're reading intently. The 10-10 strengthens the eye's *ciliary muscle,* a very important muscle that changes the shape of the eye lens so you can focus on nearer objects or farther objects. Here's how you do it:

1. **Look up from your reading and focus on an object that is at least 10 feet away.**

2. **Focus on the object for 10 seconds and return to your reading.**

3. **Repeat Steps 1 and 2 every 10 minutes.**

Athletes, especially baseball players, have very strong ciliary muscles in their eyes. They have to be able to track a fast-moving ball as it moves from a distance to points closer and closer to their bodies. Imagine for a minute that you're a batter watching a pitch come toward you or you're an outfielder watching a fly ball come your way. You can feel the ciliary muscles in your eyes changing shape.

Change of Focus

Like the 10-10-10 in the preceding section, this exercise increases the strength and flexibility of the ciliary muscles used in focusing. After age 40, you lose 10 percent of the strength in your ciliary muscles every year, so this exercise is especially good for people in their fourth decade and beyond. Follow these steps:

1. **Hold your index finger five or six inches in front of your nose and focus on your fingernail for about 5 seconds until you can see it clearly.**

2. **Over about 5 seconds, slowly move your focus to an object eight or ten feet in front of you and focus on it until you see it clearly.**

3. **Slowly move your focus back to your thumbnail over about 5 seconds.**

4. **Repeat Steps 2 and 3 ten times.**

Palming

Palming is a technique for resting the eyes. When duty calls and you must keep reading in spite of tired eyes, take a 3- to 5-minute break and practice this technique. Your eyes will thank you for it.

You can also rest your neck and shoulders while palming.

1. **Rub your palms together to warm them.**

2. **Place your bent elbows on your desk or table and cup your hands with your palms facing toward you.**

3. **Close your eyes and slowly lower your eyes and head onto the palms of your hands, trying to keep any light from penetrating between your fingers.**

4. **Breathing slowly, rest on your cupped hands for 3 to 5 minutes without applying pressure to your eyeballs, and think of a happy occurrence or beautiful place.**

Hooded Eyes

Hooded eyes is another technique for relaxing your eyes; do this exercise two or three times when your eyes need a quick timeout.

1. **Close your eyes halfway and concentrate on stopping your eyelids from trembling.**

    As you concentrate on your eyelids, you're really relaxing your eyes.

2. **With your eyes still half closed, gaze at a faraway object.**

    Your eyes stop trembling.

Eye Massage

You've probably tried this one before. Massaging the eyes is as good for the eyeballs as a shoulder or neck massage is for those areas. But easy does it — you're not doing a Swedish massage or anything.

1. **Close your eyes.**

2. **Gently roll your fingertips over your eyelids, massaging your eyes for a moment or two until they start to relax.**

Don't press too hard! While you're at it, you may give your temples and forehead a light massage.

Chapter 16

Ten Tips for Making Your Speed-Reading Skills Permanent

To be a speed reader, you have to keep your speed-reading skills up to snuff. Unless you sharpen your skills, they erode over time. This brief chapter is for people who have become speed readers and want to prevent their speed-reading skills from slipping. It explains a handful of actions you can take to make your speed-reading skills permanent.

Renew Your Commitment

Speed reading is more than just a matter of acquiring speed-reading techniques. You also have to make the commitment to being a speed reader, and after you become a speed reader, renew your commitment from time to time.

Tell yourself, "I want to read faster and get more out of my reading," and then think of steps you can take to reach this goal:

✔ Don't vocalize when you read. (See Chapter 2 for more on vocalizing.)

✔ Make a conscious commitment to read more than one word at a time. Chapter 6 gives you the skinny on reading in clumps.

✔ Read with more concentration.

✔ Expand your vision span so you can take in more words when you read. Chapter 6 can help you out here as well.

Expand Your Reading Vision

To make your speed-reading skills permanent, continue to expand your reading vision by using the guidelines in Chapter 6. As Chapter 3 explains in loving detail, your eyes fixate on words or groups of words in the act of reading. As you read from left to right across the page, your eyes take in 1 to 14 words at a time. The more words you can read at once, the faster you can read.

Keep working at taking in more words at once. When you come to the end of one line, don't swing your eyes to the start of the next line. Move to a place partway into the next line and start reading there. Similarly, don't read to the end of each line — try to take in the last four to five words without moving your eyes to the end of the line.

Shush Your Inner Reading Voice

Because I can't say it enough, I'm going to say it again: To be a speed reader, you must silence your inner reading voice. You must cultivate the habit of reading without hearing your own voice recite the words.

Dropping the vocalization habit (discussed in Chapter 2) is the first big hurdle you must cross to become a speed reader, and you have to keep that persistent voice quiet for continued success.

When you're actively engaged in speed reading and you hear the voice, make a conscientious effort to suppress it. Focus on the shapes of words. Try to process the words and take in their meaning with your visual faculties only.

Read More Often

If you want your speed-reading skills to be permanent, you have to make reading a part of your daily life. When you read more often, you acquire more vocabulary words and therefore become a faster reader. Because your vocabulary is larger, you don't have to stop as often to ponder what a word you don't know means.

Reading more often also increases your breadth of knowledge, and that in turn increases your reading speed. For example, you don't have to stop to think about background information because you already know it from your previous reading.

Rather than watch TV before you go to bed, read a book or magazine. Your dreams will be sweeter, I assure you.

Be a Goal-Oriented Reader

No matter what the endeavor, your chances of succeeding are better if you set goals for yourself. This fact of life is why speed readers set goals for themselves when they read. If you ask yourself, "Why am I reading this and what do I want to get from this reading?" before you start reading a book or article, you're able to read much more aggressively.

Asking that simple question makes your reading much more productive because you establish goals when you read. As you read along, you can skim or skip material that doesn't help you reach your goals. And if you come to paragraphs that get to the heart of why you're reading, you can read those paragraphs more carefully and get more out of your reading. Chapter 10 helps you figure out how to get what you need and get out.

Enlarge Your Vocabulary

To continue to be a speed reader, you must always work to enlarge your vocabulary. The larger your vocabulary is, the faster you can read because you don't have to stop and ponder as many unknown words.

Chapter 12 explains how you acquire new words and how to actively seek out vocab expansion. It also presents common prefixes, roots, and suffixes to help you decode new words as you encounter them.

Be a Strategic Reader

Above and beyond reading mechanics, you must continue to refine your strategic reading abilities if you want to be a long-term speed reader. For example, you must read word groups and thought units, not words alone (see Chapter 7). Another helpful habit: Become a *bird's-eye view reader* — instead of burying your nose in the pages, read from on high, noting such points as how the author is makes her argument and whether you can skim or skip certain paragraphs (or even the entire work). Chapters 10 and 11 cover the habits of these wily readers.

Occasionally Time Yourself

You can tell for certain whether your speed-reading skills are eroding by timing yourself when you read. Chapter 5 offers a test to measure your reading speed (and Appendix B has a place for recording your scores on this test). From time to time, take the test in Chapter 5 to see whether your reading speed is decreasing or increasing. If you find yourself slipping, try to determine why and then brush up on the appropriate skills.

Do Your Exercises

I hope you complete all the exercises in this book on your way to becoming a speed reader. And I recommend doing the exercises again to keep up your speed-reading skills. In fact, I recommend doing the exercises again and again and again.

For that matter, next time you're reading a newspaper, book, or magazine, pretend you're doing a speed-reading test. Apply all you know about speed reading to the text in front of you. See whether you can tackle your newspaper article, book chapter, or magazine article like a tried-and-true speed reader.

Visit the Optometrist

Your ability to speed read is only as good as your ability to see words on the page. If you aren't yet 40, you're in for a surprise where your eyes are concerned (and if you're over 40, you probably know what I'm talking about).

Starting around age 40, your eyesight starts to deteriorate. You have trouble reading small print. You have to hold the menu farther and farther from your face as the years go by, until by age 50 your arm isn't long enough and you end up with stew when you thought you ordered steak.

To avoid such culinary disasters and keep your speed reading up to par, have your eyes checked regularly after the age of 40, and get yourself a pair of glasses if necessary. You can't speed read without them. If your peepers are already healthy, thank your lucky stars and then keep them that way with the eye exercises in Chapter 15.

Part VI
Appendixes

"It's the free gift I got with my speed-reading course. A microwave slow cooker."

In this part...

You've found them — the appendixes stashed away at the end of this book. Appendix A lists the 2,000 most common words in the English language; these words represent about 75 percent of the words you encounter in your reading, so knowing them can greatly increase your reading speed and comprehension. Appendix B is a worksheet for tracking your scores on the exercises in this book.

Appendix A

Uncovering the Prime Words

• •

*T*his appendix lists prime words and discusses how these common words can improve your vocabulary (an essential speed-reading tool) and put you on the fast track to speedy reading. It also lists these 2,000 words so you can get cracking.

Discovering Prime Words

To find out what the most commonly used words are, my company, The Literacy Company, downloaded all the books available on Project Gutenberg (www.gutenberg.org), the online digital library consisting of more than 13,000 books (about 548 million words altogether). We entered all the books in a database and then queried the database to find out the 2,000 most popular words.

I call these words *prime words* because they're the primary words you encounter in your reading. Based on our experiment with Project Guttenberg, these prime words represent 75 percent of all the words in the English language. That means that you can master the prime words and rest assured that you know 75 percent of the vocabulary words you need in your reading.

After you get the prime words down, your reading comprehension, retention, and recall increase because knowing the prime words gives you these advantages in your reading:

✔ You recognize the words immediately, so you don't have to decode them.

✔ Your eyes don't fixate on the words (so you can read them as part of word groups).

Prime Words List

Following are lists of the 2,000 prime words divided into 10 groups of about 200 words per group. Group 1 lists the most common prime words; group 10 lists the least common.

Read this list to make sure that you know all the prime words. When you come to a word you don't know, circle it, and go back and research the circled words to get their meanings. You may have to look up the words you circled in a dictionary.

Although this book is about speed reading, don't feel like you have sit down and cram a bunch of unfamiliar words into your brain this afternoon. The way to eat an elephant is one bite a time, so take out your fork and tackle these prime words in whatever manageable chunks work for you.

Group 1

a, about, after, again, against, all, also, am, among, an, and, another, any, are, as, at, away, back, be, because, been, before, being, but, by, came, can, children, come, could, day, did, do, done, down, each, even, ever, every, eyes, face, father, first, for, found, from, get, give, go, god, good, great, had, hand, has, have, he, head, heard, heart, her, here, him, himself, his, house, how, I, if, in, into, is, it, it's, just, know, land, last, left, let, life, like, little, long, look, looked, lord, made, make, man, many, may, me, men, might, more, most, Mr., Mrs., much, must, my, name, never, new, night, no, not, nothing, now, of, off, old, on, once, one, only, or, other, our, out, over, own, party, people, place, put, rate, right, said, same, saw, say, see, seemed, shall, she, should, side, since, so, some, son, still, such, take, tell, than, that, the, their, them, then, there, these, they, thing, things, think, this, those, though, thought, three, through, time, to, too, took, total, two, under, unto, up, upon, us, very, was, way, we, well, went, were, what, when, where, which, while, who, why, will, with, without, world, would, years, yet, you, young, your

Group 2

above, according, age, air, almost, alone, along, always, answered, anything, area, asked, began, behind, behold, believe, best, better, between, billion, black, body, both, branch, bring, brought, call, called, cannot, certain, change, chapter, child, city, coming, country, course, cried, days, dead, dear, death, does, door, earth, end, enough, far, fear, feel, feet, fell, felt, few, find, fire, five, force, form, forth, four, friend, full, gave, general, girl, given, going, gone, got, government, ground, growth, half, hands, having, hear, heaven, held, help, herself, high, home, hope, hour, however, hundred, including, indeed, Israel, keep, kind, knew, known, labor, large, law, lay, least, less, light, live, looking, love, matter, million, mind, mine, miss, moment, money, morning, mother, myself, national, natural, near, neither, next, none, note, often, oh, open, others, part, pass, passed, per, perhaps, person, point, poor, population, power, project, quite, rather, read, red, replied, rest, return, room, round, sat, saying, sea, second, seen, sent, set, sight, sir, small, something, soon, sort, soul, speak, state, states, stood, sure, system, taken, themselves, therefore, thousand, thus, till, times, together, told, toward, towards, true, turn, turned, until, use, used, voice, want, water, whether, white, whole, whom, whose, wife, wish, within, woman, women, word, words, work, year, yes

Group 3

able, across, added, agriculture, already, answer, appeared, arm, arms, around, art, ask, bad, bear, beautiful, became, become, bed, beyond, big, birth, blood, blue, book, boy, brother, business, capital, captain, care, carried, case, cast, cause, certainly, chief, close, cold, common, constitution, continued, council, countries, court, cut, dark, daughter, deep, defense, die, different, doubt, during, eat, economic, economy, either, else, English, entered, evening, everything, evil, except, exchange, expenditures, eye, fact, fall, family, feeling, female, fine, followed, following, food, forest, free, French, friends, front, further, gold, green, hair, happy, hard, hold, holy, hours, human, husband, idea, information, interest, island, islands, itself, Jerusalem, July, kept, lady, laid, leave, legal, letter, line, living, longer, lost, low, making, male, manner, master, mean, means, military, minister, mouth, nature, need, north, number, ocean, oil, opened, order, ought, parties, past, peace, plain, political, possible, present, president, pretty, public, question, reached, ready, real, really, reason, received, remember, republic, returned, river, road, rose, run, runways, saith, save, says, send, sense, service, services, seven, several, ship, short, six, sometimes, sons, sound, south, spirit, stand, strange, street, strength, strong, subject, suddenly, sun, suppose, table, taking, talk, ten, tom, town, tree, trees, truth, understand, united, walk, walked, wall, wanted, war, whale, window, won, yea

Group 4

account, act, afraid, ago, aid, angel, army, article, attention, battle, beginning, below, beneath, beside, births, books, branches, bread, broken, caught, chance, Christian, church, claims, clear, commanded, company, corner, creature, crops, cry, darkness, deal, deaths, december, democratic, desire, died, direction, distance, divisions, doctor, doing, drew, drink, early, east, effect, Egypt, escape, exclaimed, executive, fair, faith, fathers, fellow, field, figure, filled, fish, fit, flag, flesh, floor, follow, foot, forces, former, forward, France, garden, gate, getting, glad, glory, goods, greater, happened, hardly, heavy, horse, hot, immediately, includes, independence, indian, industrial, instant, instead, international, iron, January, joy, judge, knowledge, language, late, later, leaders, led, legislative, length, lips, lived, mac, Madame, March, Mary, meet, members, met, midst, mighty, minutes, month, moved, nations, nearly, necessary, net, offering, outside, paper, particular, pay, persons, places, please, pleasure, presence, presently, priest, produced, production, products, provided, purpose, raised, ran, reach, receive, remained, resources, seats, secret, seeing, seem, seems, servant, servants, show, silence, silver, single, sister, sit, sleep, slowly, smile, spake, spoke, spoken, standing, stations, stay, stone, stopped, story, struck, surely, sword, tariff, telephone, territory, thinking, third, thoughts, top, trade, tried, trouble, try, turning, twenty, type, union, value, view, wait, west, western, wild, wind, wood, works, write, written, wrong, yellow, yourself

Group 5

accounts, address, administrative, afternoon, although, appearance, assembly, authority, bank, based, beast, begin, bit, boat, born, bottom, bound, box, break, breath, bright, capacity, carry, central, chair, chamber, character, cities, civil, clock, closed, comes, command, commitments, communications, concerning, consumer, copy, covered, danger, debt, diplomatic, directly, dollars, dropped, dry, duty, ears, easy, embassy, enemy, England, enter, entirely, environment, equal, established, exactly, expected, exports, external, fallen, fast, fifty, fight, fixed, foreign, fresh, fruit, future, gas, gathered, gentleman, girls, grew, group, guard, happiness, heading, heads, hill, important, imports, impossible, industry, item, journey, judgment, judicial, June, jungle, justice, kill, kingdom, knows, latter, laughed, lead, leaving, lie, lion, London, loved, lower, major, makes, maritime, married, meant, meat, member, middle, miles, minute, months, moon, mountains, movement, names, nobody, notice, November, object, occupied, October, offer, office, opinion, otherwise, paid, parts, percent, perfect, permanent, petroleum, piece, placed, play, position, pray, prepared, prices, prime, prince, print, probably, queen, quickly, quiet, race, remain, representation, respect, rich, saint, sake, school, seek, ships, shut, signs, silent, sin, sitting, sky, slightly, speaking, spot, start, started, stop, straight, stranger, sudden, supreme, sweet, talking, tears, terrible, today, tone, trust, trying, usual, village, waiting, watch, waters, ways, week, whatever, wicked, wide, wine, wise, wished, wonder, worse, worth, youth

Group 6

American, ancient, animal, appear, April, arable, Atlantic, aunt, beauty, believed, besides, bird, blessed, boundaries, boys, broad, broke, budget, built, Canada, cargo, caused, changed, charge, circumstances, climate, clothes, coast, coastline, comparative,

consider, considered, conversation, cost, cotton, currency,
delivered, determined, development, discovered, drawn,
dream, dress, dwell, ear, easily, edge, eight, elections, enemies,
equipment, especially, ethnic, Europe, everybody, experience,
expression, faces, fanny, February, federal, feelings, finally, fishing,
flowers, formed, freckles, geography, giving, glass, grave, hall,
hat, hearts, history, horses, houses, huge, ill, industries, infant,
inflation, Japan, kings, knowing, laugh, laws, learn, learned, letters,
level, lifted, likely, lines, lives, local, lot, mark, marriage, marry,
materials, meadows, medium, memory, mercy, mere, merely,
method, Mexico, move, narrow, nation, neck, nevertheless, noise,
observed, occasion, offered, official, ones, opportunity, overview,
Pacific, pain, passing, pastures, path, perfectly, period, plan,
pleasant, ports, priests, private, program, provide, quick, rain,
rates, request, required, result, results, revenues, rise, rising,
running, safe, sand, seat, September, shadow, shook, shoulder,
showed, sign, simple, sing, size, social, society, soft, sorry, sought,
space, spirits, spread, spring, step, steps, summer, surprise,
talked, telecommunications, temple, terrain, territorial, thank,
thirty, tomorrow, touch, transport, twelve, uncle, unemployment,
universal, unless, upper, vain, valley, various, visit, walls, warm,
Washington, watched, wilderness, wisdom, York, zone

Group 7

action, advantage, Africa, aircraft, agreement, airports, alive,
allow, allowed, altar, ambassador, America, anger, angry, anybody,
arose, arrived, aside, association, attempt, awful, band, bare,
beasts, begun, bent, bilateral, blow, board, building, burnt, camp,
center, choose, coat, college, comfort, commodities, communist,
content, conversion, copyright, creatures, cross, curious, date,
degree, deliver, destroy, difference, difficult, dinner, disputes,
dog, domestic, draw, drive, due, electricity, engaged, evidently,
example, existence, expectancy, fancy, fate, fertility, file, fingers,
finished, fiscal, flat, fool, forget, forgotten, forty, generally, glance,
gods, goes, golden, grace, grand, grass, groups, guess, highways,
holding, holiday, host, hung, imagine, influence, intended, Internet,
keeping, killed, leaves, liberty, limited, literacy, looks, lose, lying,
matters, meaning, measure, merchant, migration, moreover,
mortality, mostly, mount, multitude, music, nationality, news,
noble, oak, obliged, opposite, ourselves, pale, Paris, partners,
passage, picture, pieces, pleased, possession, powers, praise,
pride, product, professor, promise, proper, property, questions,
reading, regard, religion, repeated, reply, rights, rock, rule, savage,
saved, scarcely, scene, search, season, seed, serious, serve,
sharp, sheep, shot, shoulders, similar, simply, situation, smoke,
softly, special, speech, spent, standard, statement, station, stones,
streets, subheading, suffrage, supposed, surface, tall, teeth, terror,

text, thick, threw, throne, tongue, tribe, TV, twice, understanding, understood, vast, vote, waited, walking, watching, weight, wonderful, woodland, working, wrote

Group 8

accepted, afterwards, agree, agricultural, altogether, apply, appointed, articles, August, author, base, beheld, birds, blind, bow, breakfast, breast, British, brown, bulk, buried, burst, cabinet, carriage, catch, cattle, ceased, characters, China, chosen, class, clean, clearly, colonel, companion, complete, computer, condition, conduct, confidence, congregation, congress, considerable, construction, countenance, courage, crowd, crude, dare, daughters, decided, deck, delight, departed, destroyed, devil, difficulty, distribute, doesn't, domain, doors, double, dressed, drop, dust, effort, empty, ended, excellent, expect, families, files, fled, forced, fortune, gauge, German, Germany, governor, greatest, greatly, grow, growing, grown, happen, hate, hearing, higher, hills, hurt, image, inhabitants, inside, languages, larger, legs, lies, liked, list, listen, listened, loss, loud, machine, machinery, males, marine, measures, meeting, meter, Mexican, migrants, mountain, moving, named, network, nice, nine, noticed, occurred, officers, opening, organized, original, palace, particularly, personal, pity, police, possibly, princess, prison, prisoner, progress, proud, pure, putting, quarter, remembered, removed, righteousness, royal, rue, sacrifice, sad, safety, satisfied, Saul, sector, seized, shame, shape, share, sick, sides, singular, smiled, somewhat, sorrow, speed, spite, square, stars, stretched, study, suffer, sufficient, support, surprised, taste, taught, telephones, telling, term, terms, thin, throughout, throw, thrown, tired, tonight, touched, train, units, unknown, usable, using, usually, weather, weeks, whispered, wilt, windows, winter, wore, worked, worthy, writing, yards, yours

Group 9

accept, acts, actually, advance, advanced, affairs, affection, agreed, ahead, anxious, apes, approached, Arab, arise, armed, ashamed, asleep, Australia, avenue, aware, bands, bearing, beat, bodies, bore, buy, cabin, calendar, Canadian, carefully, cases, Catholic, claim, cloud, coffee, comfortable, conditions, consulate, continental, control, corn, couple, covenant, crossed, crown, cruel, daily, declared, depth, described, desert, destruction, direct, disappeared, disk, distant, divided, dozen, drawing, dreadful, driven, dwelt, ease, efforts, entire, equivalent, escaped, exclusive, expense, explain, explained, faint, false, farther, fault, feared, features, final, finding, flight, forms, fully, gates, gentle, gentlemen, gray, handsome, harm, haven, health, hell, hid, hide, highest, honest, honor, hosts, ideas, independent, India, iniquity, instance, instantly, interested, interesting, irrigated, Italy, joined, key, knees, knight, ladies, lake, mad, main, manpower, marked, mass, material, modern, moments, nearer, necessity, nose, orders, origin, paused, peculiar, perceived, physical, played, pocket, pointed, points, popular, portion, powerful, precious, prepare, pressure, prevent, price, princes, principal, processing, produce, promised, prophet, prophets, prove, proved, quietly, radio, raise, rapidly, reign, righteous, rolled, Roman, seated, section, security, separate, sergeant, served, settled, shore, sins, skin, slain, slight, slow, smaller, software, souls, sprang, steel, success, suffered, suggested, tanker, tea, teach, therein, thyself, tropical, truly, vessels, vice, visible, vision, waste, weak, wings, witness, wondered, woods, workers, wrath, yesterday

Group 10

absolutely, acquaintance, activity, add, additional, admit, African, animals, annex, annually, apparently, approach, attack, Babylon, beloved, bless, border, bowed, brain, build, burning, calling, calm, carrying, CD, chairman, chancery, charity, chemicals, choice, circle, clothing, clouds, commandments, completely, conscience, contrary, cool, counsel, cousin, created, crew, curiosity, damages, dance, description, desired, despair, developed, discover, dollar, eastern, elected, electronic, energy, entrance, equally, evidence, express, extent, fail, failed, faithful, falling, familiar, fashion, fat, fields, fierce, figures, finger, fix, fly, fond, foolish, fourth, freedom, frightened, gain, game, gather, gently, ghost, gravel, heat, heavens, height, helped, hence, hidden, hideous, highly, hole, hoped, horrible, horror, Illinois, imagination, include, increase, increased, inheritance, inland, interests, interior, investment, jurisdiction, kindness, kitchen, knife, laughing, leading, library, location, loose, lovely, mailing, market, mentioned, minds, ministers, miserable, misery, mistake, mistress, murmured, native, navy, needs, Netherlands, northern, numerous, ordinary, organization, page, papers, passion, possess, possessed, post, pounds, prayer, presented, process, pulled, rage, railroads, reasons, recognized, regular, relief, remains, report, representatives, roads, roof, scarlet, scattered, shadows, shelf, shew, slept, smote, snow, soil, soldiers, somebody, song, sounds, southern, spare, stepped, storm, stream, strike, suffering, sugar, Sunday, supper, tabernacle, takes, temper, tender, textiles, thanks, throat, thrust, timber, track, vessel, voices, wants, warn, warriors, wear, welcome, whenever, wherein, willing, yourselves

Appendix B

Your Speed-Reading Progress Worksheet

• •

*T*his appendix is a worksheet that you can use to track your progress on various exercises in this book. It also explains how to calculate your WPM (word-per-minute) reading rate and your ERR (effective reading rate) for any given reading selection.

Calculating Your WPM Rate and ERR

Some of the exercises in this book ask you to calculate your WPM reading rate and your ERR. Chapter 5 explains these rates in detail; you can use the following formulas to calculate them.

Use this formula to calculate your WPM (word-per-minute) reading rate:

_____ Number of words in the reading selection

÷ _____ Time to read the reading selection (enter fractions of minutes as decimals)

= _____ WPM

Use this formula to calculate your ERR (effective reading rate):

_____ WPM rate

× _____ Percentage of comprehension questions answered correctly (enter as a decimal)

= _____ ERR

Speed Reading Progress Worksheet

Use this worksheet to enter your scores for exercises in this book.
I recommend doing these exercises more than once, and for that
reason, I have included places for recording more than one score
by date for each test. Some exercises in this book don't require
you to enter scores in this worksheet, and I didn't include places
here for recording your scores on those exercises.

Practice Text 1-1

Date	1st reading time	2nd reading time

Practice Text 2-1

Date	1st reading time	2nd reading time

Practice Text 3-1

Date	1st reading time	2nd reading time

Practice Text 4-1

Date	Correct score	Incorrect score

Practice Text 4-3

Date	Time to complete exercise

Practice Text 4-7

Date	Block WPM rate	Column WPM rate	Block ERR	Column ERR

Practice Text 5-1

Date	WPM rate	ERR

Practice Text 5-2

Date	WPM rate	ERR

Practice Text 8-1

Date	WPM rate	ERR

Practice Text 8-2

Date	WPM rate	ERR

Practice Text 8-3

Date	WPM rate	ERR

Practice Text 8-4

Date	WPM rate	ERR

Practice Text 9-1

Date	Line reached in 60 seconds	Line reached in 50 seconds

Practice Text 9-2

Date	Line reached in 60 seconds	Line reached in 50 seconds

Practice Text 11-1

Date	Sentences 1–10 time	Sentences 11–20 time

Index

A Special Offer for You!

Congratulations! You've taken the first step to improving your reading speed, comprehension, retention, and recall.

To help maintain and further improve your newly acquired reading skills, I've arranged a special offer: 20 percent off The Reader's Edge®, The Literacy Company's top-rated speed-reading software.

With automated training exercises and real-time feedback, The Reader's Edge® provides a great way for you and your family to continue your training.

To learn more about this exciting program and to save **20 percent** on your order, go to

www.FluentReading.com/DummiesOffer

For Dummies is a registered trademark of John Wiley & Sons, Inc. and its affiliates.

Do More with Dummies

Products for the Rest of Us!

DVDs • Music • Games • DIY • Crafts
Consumer Electronics • Software
Hobbies • Cookware • and more!

3 1901 05308 7211

Check out the Dummies Product Shop at www.dummies.com for more information!

 **WILEY**